Sarah Tytler

Scotch Marriages

Vol. 3

Sarah Tytler

Scotch Marriages
Vol. 3

ISBN/EAN: 9783337408909

Printed in Europe, USA, Canada, Australia, Japan

Cover: Foto ©Suzi / pixelio.de

More available books at **www.hansebooks.com**

SCOTCH MARRIAGES

BY

SARAH TYTLER

AUTHOR OF
'SCOTCH FIRS' 'CITOYENNE JACQUELINE' &c.

IN THREE VOLUMES

VOL. III.

LONDON
SMITH, ELDER, & CO., 15 WATERLOO PLACE
1882

CONTENTS

OF

THE THIRD VOLUME.

'HAMESUCKEN'

(CONTINUED).

CHAPTER		PAGE
VII.	LIFE AT BIRKENCRAIG	3
VIII.	BRUCE LOCKS THE KIRK DOOR ON THE MINISTER	29
IX.	THE RED-CROSS AMBULANCE CLASS . .	60
X.	'HAMESUCKEN'	100
XI.	THE MINISTER 'WAITED UPON' . . .	131
XII.	'TIRLING AT THE PIN' . . .	173
XIII.	THE END OF THE HONEYMOON . .	212

'HAMESUCKEN.'

(CONTINUED).

CHAPTER VII.

LIFE AT BIRKENCRAIG.

The household at Birkencraig, from Miss Kirkpatrick the eldest member to the youngest yawning housemaid, lounged and dawdled out of bed at a late hour in the morning. It was an exception to this rule that once or twice in the year, whether it was summer or winter was a wholly inconsequent matter, Bruce, in a fit of superfluous energy, got up with the cock-crowing, and either went on enterprising excursions through the sleeping house to the pantry and dairy to supply her pressing wants, or fasted for half a dozen hours to the injury of her bodily well-being and her temper. She made up for the rare exertion by over-sleeping herself on nearly every other day of the three hundred and sixty-four days which were left.

The breakfast would be standing on the table at Birkencraig with the work of the day hardly begun, after the family at the Manse of Birkenbarns had dined with their day and its duties half over. But the lingering breakfast was not the ladies' fault; the culprit was Claud, who, after what he called 'a beastly bad night,' would stroll to the kennel and the stables in his slippers between two and three o'clock in the afternoon.

The elder Misses Kirkpatrick always spent the greater part of their day, doubtless with a reference to the chilly climate of Scotland, in voluminous shawls and caps. The last were more of a shelter than any bonnets, always excepting Mary and Lily Kirkpatrick's bonnets, which they wore on a corresponding principle. These, Bruce said, might have been hung up in a museum as specimens of out-of-doors' headgear for use, not show, belonging to antediluvians. The sisters had in their day been fond enough of smart clothes, not always in the best taste though the clothes were worn by gentle-folks and county people, witness the tradition of the pea-green satin pelisse associated with Miss Lily's young beauty, and the rose-pink ball gown equally linked with the morning glories of Miss Kirkpatrick's charms. Now the sisters went in for comfort, pure and unalloyed, in extreme dowdiness, which was just saved from more reprehensible slovenliness by the fact that those who practised it had been reared in such of those laws of delicate personal cleanliness and nicety of surroundings as had reached their class forty or fifty years ago. Neither could any smothering, huddling together wraps altogether hide and disfigure the remains of the Kirkpatrick beauty. It had reached the stage of matronly bountifulness, though neither of the two was a matron, and could successfully carry a weight of drapery. Deep borders flapping over the ears, and broad riband bows filling up the space beneath the chin, were powerless to affect the flowery fairness and purity of colouring, and the fine lines of nose and chin, which had no affinity to nut-crackers, and remained intact after the contour of brow and cheek was spoilt. Perhaps it was a proud innate consciousness of the inability of dress to rob them of what survived of the family beauty, which made the elder Misses Kirkpatrick so very elderly, unfashionable, and devoted to ease in their attire. But it is more probable that it was careless indifference to appearances, in a rebound from the love of admiration to the holding fast of comfort, rather than keen discriminating vanity, which actuated the pair. It was a relief to Bruce, who was quickly alive to the sources of conspicuousness and absurdity in her sisters, that since Mary and Lily would be such 'old wives' in their costumes, they could not help being bonnie old wives.

Other reactions from what had been, presented themselves at the Birkencraig breakfast-table. The old laird, though he had not been any more of a model than his son, had played the martinet, an inclination which in Claud's case only lingered in the strict discipline he was inclined to enforce on his sister Bruce, with unfair capriciousness, as it seemed to her. The father of the family, a selfish, self-indulgent man after his fashion, had prided himself on displaying punctuality in his own person and exacting it from others. So long as he ruled the roost, the breakfast-table was cleared by half-past ten whatever laggard suffered. In all table etiquette he was precise and particular in private as in public. Nicol, the butler, waited behind his master's chair, when only the family were there, as duly and decorously as when the meet came round to Birkencraig and Mr. Kirkpatrick dispensed the hunting breakfast, or when the house was full of company about the first of September. Mary, who had always sat opposite her father at table after her mother's death, dare not let a cup get out of its place, or drop a lump of sugar, whoever were at her elbow whispering soft nothings in her ear. Lily could not give a scrap to a dog though her four-footed friends begged and whimpered their hearts out. Now all was changed. Nicol chose the breakfast hour for reading the newspapers before they had reached anyone else, and systematically absented himself if the presence of strangers did not make an urgent appeal to his sense of honour for the credit of the house, or unless Claud summoned and swore over him for not having supplied something the young man fancied he wanted.

Miss Kirkpatrick seated herself according to the temperature of the room or the direction of the wind, and pulled about or allowed others to pull about the different articles on the table till everything was in a state of admired confusion, liable to end in the cream-jug's being overturned or the coffee-pot capsized.

Lily not only fed her dogs, she opened the French windows when the season would permit, and enticed in long-legged, long-necked cocks and hens lying in wait outside. These invaders sprawled up the table and pecked promiscuously at any food they could reach. Pigeons followed, and whirling round the heads of the circle alighted in the centre, and dabbed right and left with short abrupt pecks. Bruce often protested she might as well breakfast in a menagerie, but it was only when Claud's step was heard coming downstairs that the feathered retainers were driven out.

The most energetic, enterprising person— and Bruce was naturally energetic and enterprising—could hardly help growing lazy and purposeless at Birkencraig, where it was time to think of lunch before breakfast had vanished, and it was not worth while so much as to propose practising, or reading, or working—at so-called work, in the short interval. Mary and Lily, indeed, generally sauntered off by turns, for one always mounted guard at the table, amongst the wrecks of the meal, to look after Claud's comforts and listen to his querulous complaints and demands. This was an important duty which could not be left to an inattentive, impatient child like Bruce. The sentry off duty went no farther than the housekeeper's room, or the green-houses, or the poultry yard, where, to the accompaniment of a perennial broad stream of gossip, a trickle of business was distilled drop by drop, in the familiar, half-clattering, half-drowsy scene. Miss Kirkpatrick made out the dinner to the satisfaction of Mattie, the short in stature, short in wind, but long-tongued old housekeeper and cook, who was as homely as Nicol was pompous. Yet she closely resembled him in this respect, that she had not the slightest idea of doing anything but taking her own way, always saving where the young master's flights and furies were concerned.

In spite of Claud, who had no strength of character or capacity to rule in his self-will and passion, Liberty Hall had been established at Birkencraig to a great extent from the date of the old laird's failing health and death; and the servants, whose places had become sinecures, while their perquisites were established privileges, showed themselves determined, so far as it lay with them, to prolong this agreeable state of matters indefinitely.

Lily would over-feed her feathered friends a little more till they began to bluster and brawl and knocked the plate or basket out of her hands, and fought among her feet for the last remnants of her generous largesses. She would imagine she was cutting clusters of grapes, or pulling nectarines, or gathering camellias as she chose, when she was in reality humbly suggesting that she or Miss Kirkpatrick or Miss Bruce or the Laird would like one or two, and having them doled out to her by the grumbling lame gardener, who had fallen off a ladder in the family's service twenty years before, and traded on the accident to this day. The dole was bestowed with a grudging sparingness, which was in broad contrast to her own liberal donations to her dogs, cats, and fowls.

If any further business were done, it was in a series of interviews sought by the ladies' pensioners, and never denied them; indeed, it would have been difficult to say who would have lost most by the denial. The pauperised, gadding, chattering claimants would walk a mile or two to Birkencraig on the excuse of getting an old pair of boots or stockings, a bundle of 'odds and ends'—as often old trashy finery as anything else, an apron full of broken meat or fallen apples, a glass of ginger wine. Mattie and Nicol took care nothing better should be got, and all of these the recipients could have done as well or a great deal better without, or they might have procured equivalents without any great trouble to themselves, while not one was worth the work forsaken for its sake.

On the other hand, the Misses Kirkpatrick were free and almost bound to enter into all the minutiæ of their clients' private histories, and to become the confidantes of a hundred secrets, which fed the simple ladies' sense of self-importance, and stirred and diverted them more than the fictitious adventures of the hero and heroine of the most sensational romance —the only romance they cared for.

Sometimes Bruce, for want of anything better to do, hung about the house and grounds with one or other of her sisters, when she would either be sarcastic and scornful of the day of such very small things, or she would have fits of remorse for her superciliousness, when she would tell herself with truth that Mary and Lily were far better than she was. They acted up to their light, they were always contented and good-natured, and they were for some good in the world, while she was for none, if she were not for evil like Claud.

Visitors and visiting belonged to the hours after lunch. Miss Kirkpatrick and Miss Lily sometimes sat in their morning gowns in the drawing-room knitting or crocheting endless clumsy coarse pieces of knitting or crochet—either charity slop-work or ornamental slop-work, which taxed neither their eyes nor their attention, and could have been done far better and in a tithe of the time by any brisk old woman or smart school-board girl in the parish. The ladies waited at home for any chance caller—generally some elderly lady like themselves, who clung to old acquaintances and an old house on her visiting list. With her the hostesses went cheerfully into the better class gossip of the neighbourhood.

At other times the sisters drove out in their warmest out-of-door wraps in the somewhat battered family phaeton and paid return visits. The seniors of the house welcomed five o'clock tea after these strenuous efforts—as heartily as if the refreshment had been well worked for and abundantly deserved.

Miss Kirkpatrick and Miss Lily still went through the form of dressing for dinner, though it was becoming more and more of a bore to them, and their soft cosy morning shawls and equally soft cosy morning caps kept intruding in place of fluttering fly-away lace shawls, and caps which were certainly more appropriate in company with the silk gowns.

So far this was Birkencraig life untroubled by Claud, and even so far it was a drowsy, gaping, wearisome life for a young girl, especially a young girl of some spirit and mind. And Claud proved a fermenting element that, like bad yeast, leavened, soured, and disturbed everything without raising it into a wholesome higher stage of development. Claud came in growling to his breakfast. He tramped out and in, always bringing with him currents of crossness and perversity, swaggering and bullying throughout the morning. He would give himself out as falling to pieces—in which the miserable lad was not far wrong—and have recourse to bitters, fillips, and pick-me-ups. Thus solaced and strengthened, he would go off to sales or fairs or sporting matches instead of staying for luncheon. His temporary absence was a respite even to his devoted sisters, though it left the shadow of an anxious care in the distance. Or he would bring in to lunch company unsuitable to sit down with the ladies of the house, or with respectable women of any class, the fallen star and reprobate, Lord Sandy;

fast, foolish young farmers who aped the vices of the vicious lairds and fawned on them with the view of rising by their aid in the social scale; half put out, half blustering horse-dealers with whom Claud was for ever dabbling; still flashier, more offensive nondescript men, who wore diamond rings on not over-clean hands, and came from the large towns, meeting Claud by appointment at Birkencraig or in Sauchope. The last mentioned of these worthies had made Claud's acquaintance under Lord Sandy's auspices. The elder Misses Kirkpatrick referred to them under the vague definition of business men, though Mr. Govan, the family lawyer, was never seen in their company. Bruce, who had gone through her curriculum of novel-reading, supposed these must be the men who cheated Claud by tempting him with bargains of bad wine, bad cigars, bad guns, bad driving-harness, bad machines for the farm, bad clothes, bad everything, and who must somehow combine money-lending at illegal interest with cheating.

When such company appeared in the dining-room Bruce held up her head stiffly and scarcely opened her lips, behaving like 'a saucy baggage' as Claud asserted, proceeding to use still coarser words, in language deteriorating with the company he kept.

The elder Misses Kirkpatrick were always civil to their boy's guests, but a red spot rose and settled on each cheek and a constrained tone stole into their frank speech, uttered with voices just a little loud for women though sweet withal, as their accents were a trifle broad for ladies.

In wet weather the strange men would retire with Claud to the billiard room, where Nicol would soon be rung for to bring bottles and glasses. Cards would succeed billiards, and the noisy hubbub, which Mary and Lily would pretend not to hear, or insist on regarding as a matter of course where gentlemen were concerned, would subside into more business-like stillness. It would not be Claud's fault if the company declined to stay to dinner, with a rather slow perception of his incapacity to stand the situation much longer.

'They dare not face us,' Bruce would cry in her fiery way. 'If they did, I almost believe I must tell them what I think, after what they've done to Claud.'

'Oh! hush, Brucie,' interposed her elders, 'that would be dreadful; you would make yourself notorious. Nobody would ever let it down on you. A young girl has nothing to do with how men choose to spend their time. Besides, what have these gentlemen' ('gentlemen!' repeated Bruce with bitter emphasis) 'done to Claud? The poor boy is simply worn out. You know he is not strong, you meddlesome hard-hearted girl, he gets so excited while he is not able for excitement. He will have a sleep in his dressing-room and be all right again presently.'

Bruce did not adopt the explanation. 'I wish it would not rain when such people come here,' she said gloomily, 'though it would not matter much. There are always the poor pigeons for them to shoot at, and bet upon, or I have known somebody take off his hat and make that the aim, with the rest laying wagers on the hits and misses. Yes, and all this is such thirsty work, while there are pocket pistols which hold neither powder nor shot. Oh! I cannot profess to be a goose like you two.'

'I think it is worse to affect to be knowing,' retorted one of the others with unwonted sharpness; 'but the truth is, you are young and know nothing at all—not even that men must have sport of some kind.'

'And what must women have—women who cannot shut their eyes?' Bruce asked herself in despair.

The visiting circle of Birkencraig was always narrowing, especially where the younger members of the family were in question. There were prudent fathers and mothers who would not have Claud Kirkpatrick, reeking with the fumes of Lord Sandy's company, to come among their young sons and daughters. Because they would not have Claud, they could not well ask his sister Bruce to join their sets. There were other families not so particular, but Bruce gradually grew to hate accompanying Claud to picnics or carpet dances or lawn games, for even when he had not the opportunity of forgetting every obligation, he was sure to be capricious, quarrelsome, and rude. Insensibly Bruce became affected by the association, and took her tone from him. She, too, was capricious, and if not quarrelsome and rude, she grew flighty and sharp-tongued at her neighbours' expense. She began to be spoken of and shunned as ' that odd disagreeable girl,

Bruce Kirkpatrick.' It did not by any means follow that she admired Claud's manner, but she must stand by him so far as she might. She could not have him blamed alone by the ungenerous public that did not stop to make the smallest allowance for the boy's sickly constitution, defective education, and unhappy temper.

Sometimes the impulse seized on Claud to drive one or more of his sisters to Sauchope or any of the next towns to which he had innumerable errands. The offer was always received as a pleasing compliment by the elder ladies and never refused even by Bruce. But it was a compliment for which the complimented persons were secretly conscious, from the beginning, they would pay so high a price, that the pleasure—even of those who remained most resolutely blind to what was to come, was still considerably dashed with fear and trembling. The going was well enough. Claud was himself and generally in good humour then, though his good humour was never to be depended upon, and was at the best streaked with surliness. Then he drove recklessly, finding a curious stimulus and enjoyment in proportion to the apprehensions he awoke. None of the Kirkpatrick women had been born with weak nerves, and it was only the fact that Mary had once been mixed up with a terrible carriage accident, that had shaken her equanimity where driving was concerned, so that she lost colour and trembled when a horse stumbled or reared or took a corner too abruptly. This infirmity of Mary's only provoked Claud to laughter, and incited him to fresh hair-breadth exploits, if she were in the company, with her feelings ready to be victimised.

Arrived at their destination, the party separated for a time. Claud had always his own business to transact, while he would not suffer a parcel of women to look on at the transaction, as if he had continued a baby in leading-strings to his sisters, who ought to feel obliged to him for his countenance so far, in taking them out behind his 'cattle.' Therefore the ladies were left to their own devices.

After the Misses Kirkpatrick had spun out their shopping and other engagements to the utmost stretch, the ladies repaired to the hotel at which the trap and horse were put up. There followed a weary season of waiting, till the blood began to get hot or cold, the heart to throb or beat more and more slowly. Claud appeared to lose all sense of time, place, and proper conditions in the transaction of his business. The ladies would beguile the dragging hours by drinking tea, by trying to eat supper in place of dinner, with the poor prospect for elderly delicate women of driving an eight or ten miles' drive home, in an open dog-cart, and in the chill and darkness—if it were not the height of summer, when it was long past night-fall. Ears would be on the rack for hours, and the strongest nerves strained past bearing, while as a small excuse for the evident discomfort of the group, ostentatious inquiries would be made again and again about the state of the night lamps, as if the darkness were the thing most to be feared. Claud would arrive at last—but not with the overflowing though stammering apologies, the eagerness to atone, the ready penitence and sincere though fleeting regret which causes many a sweet-tempered, foolish man to be freely forgiven by the victims of his inveterate thoughtlessness and self-indulgence.

Claud Kirkpatrick would take the first word of furious scolding with what speech was left to him, and as everybody, including the landlord and hostlers, shrank from exposing him in such presence, nobody dared answer, far less contradict him. Even Bruce was silent here, with a set face and whitening lips. The sisters crept into the dog-cart and huddled themselves down in their places. Nobody ventured to remonstrate when, stumbling after them, Claud cut with his whip at the impatient horse. The landlord and his men would spring out of the way and follow to the entrance of the yard, standing looking blankly at the turn-out, as after its first violent start it went tearing down the street. Some cautious man would shake his head, some friendly spirit take the liberty of exclaiming, 'God help the poor ladies!' But who could interpose?

The horror—sometimes in part a grotesque horror, of that drive home was only known to the women, who never spoke of it even among themselves afterwards. Bruce was perfectly reticent on this point. Mary Kirkpatrick's teeth would keep chattering, and she would go on clutching deperately at the side of the dog-cart, though she contrived to refrain from maddening Claud by screaming aloud. Bruce knew that if they reached Birkencraig with their lives and without broken bones, still her eldest sister, a strong woman naturally, would remain for weeks shaken and more ailing than Lily was in these later days, in consequence of the expedition.

Claud would sway from side to side, and suddenly nod as if he were being rocked in a cradle, while Bruce would first observe by the struggling dim moonbeams or the flickering light of the lamps, when she had to run the risk of awakening him, that he had put the back of his hat foremost, like a Christy minstrel, or like a boy, 'guising' at new year, had unwittingly accomplished a moustache on one cheek by blackening it with the end of his extinguished cigar. She had a hysterical inclination to laugh, though she knew that the next moment they might all be dashed into the road or over the low parapet of the bridge they had to cross, or down the steep brae they skirted. But if God would only have mercy on their souls, a sudden, violent death might not be the worst thing which could befall them —not so great a misfortune when life was so poor and empty, so harassing, mortifying, tiresome, and joyless as it was at Birkencraig to Bruce Kirkpatrick.

CHAPTER VIII.

BRUCE LOCKS THE KIRK DOOR ON THE MINISTER.

BRUCE was not free from the extravagant love of pleasure in any form in which it presented itself to her, with the attendant disregard of consequences, which had been a marked feature in the composition of the Kirkpatricks of that and the previous generations. Perhaps the tenor of her life added to this family trait an individual inclination to snatch at every passing enjoyment and small entertainment which came in her way, and be mischievous with a shade of malice in indulging some of her fancies. Her lot was hard, or seemed so to her, and she had not at this time a fine enough character to accept the worst and make it the best in the name of her Lord and King. She had not yet forgotten or forgiven the circumstance of the minister's treating her like a child or an incapable young lady—somebody quite apart from him and Rachie. She was in danger of retaliating whenever it was in her power.

Unluckily she had soon a ludicrous chance of revenging herself for the small injury, and provoking Wat Baillie in turn—a chance of which she did not hesitate to avail herself.

Without question, ladies of all ages, women of earnest, delicate minds, should be above the boyish escapades, horse-play, and tomfoolery of practical jokes. But the elder Miss Kirkpatricks and their chosen squires had not been by any means above such simple diversion. Mary and Lily often retailed, with lingering glee, to Bruce the tricks which had been played on unsuspicious visitors and green admirers of the fair daughters of the house, even though the discovery of the pranks was sure to provoke the wrath of the laird. Birkencraig had then been full of giddy, heedless young people, who had seen livelier, less care-haunted, precarious days than any Kirkpatrick was ever likely to see again.

Bruce had listened to the stories, sometimes relishing them, sometimes thinking them silly, but not condemning them on other grounds. Now she was going to perpetrate a joke on her own account.

Bruce happened to pass the parish kirk and kirk-yard in one of her solitary walks to find the first spring orchis on the Craig, of which, like all lovers of nature in the neighbourhood, she was passionately fond. An idle impulse led her to go in and linger among the graves.

There was no sadness or even pensiveness in the act, for Bruce, though she had strong feelings, was not sentimental; at that date she was even a little hard, with the danger of getting harder in her youthful isolation and cut-and-dry philosophy. Her father, mother, and one or two baby brothers and sisters lay in a corner, in the shadow of what had once been a fine Dutch tombstone of marble showing remains of gilding. It had been brought all the way from Holland two hundred years before, as if in evidence of the comparative antiquity and former spare money of the Kirkpatricks. Bruce did not care at all for the tombstone, and thought its puffy-faced cherubs hideous. Her mother and the babies had been literally unknown to her. Her father she could recall, and he had been fond of her, with a little of Claud's capriciousness and exactions, as an old man who is not without heart is fond of the child of his age. It had been a sort of grandfatherly relation. But he had been breaking up in mind no less than in body as far back as Bruce's memory carried her. while she had been only an ignorant, unconscious child, unable to understand and bear with his infirmities. She had been frightened and repelled by many things in connection with him, and there had been natural shrinking from him as well as tenderness for him in her little heart. There had been a greater sense of relief in thinking of poor papa as released from all his ailments, and gone to be happy with mamma and her babies and the angels in heaven, than longing for him to return at the time of his death; and there was still a conviction of its being well and fit that the last and biggest mound should have been added to that cluster of mounds, which prevented all pain or even wistful yearning as Bruce gazed on the resting-place of her kindred. There was nothing to detain her there, nothing to impress, soften and sober her. She turned away to speculate composedly, even with that craving for amusement which is usually so conspicuous and so incessantly at work in youthful minds. She was in a mood to smile at every exaggerated panegyric, incongruous figure, halting verse, and bold or feeble example of spelling in the records around her. All meditations among the tombs are not so solemn as Hervey's. Boys and girls will be moved to laugh and jest there as elsewhere. It does not follow on that account that they are heartless; what says the old song:—

Werena' my heart licht, I would dee.

But for its volatility youth would never be able to bear its burdens and ripen into maturity and age. And at her most thoughtless moment, if Bruce had come across the last bed of some girl like herself, a familiar acquaintance, cut down in the spring-time of her days, if she had even encountered the record of some loss which she knew had wrung a living heart with deepest anguish, she would have been arrested and impressed for the hour. But in place of such tokens, Bruce only noticed that the kirk-door stood open, with the key hanging in the lock.

Now the kirk-yard was always open, the

gate being defended by nothing more formidable than a latch which even a child could lift. But to the credit of the children and country people who at certain seasons passed through, following a footpath which was a right of way among the graves, and led eventually by a near cut to the parish school and the village, between which and the church the school stood midway, the place was a good deal more respected than if it had been protected by bolts and bars. The sacred ground was very plain and homely, and the grass was a little tedded, with wild flowers nodding in it, but it was as fresh and free from stain as sun, wind, and rain could make it.

The only houses within sight were God's house close at hand, with an ivy screen on three of the four walls, and lichens silvering and gilding the roof, which had been left of grey stone, and the manse, with its blue slates and shining windows half hidden in its umbrageous garden. Beyond rose the wild, free Craig, which, though it belonged to a lairdship, was still in a sense nobody's land, since any vagabond or tramp could climb it and lie down and sleep among its shaggy verdure, which was not so verdant that it had not the distinct bluish purple tint which marks out virgin from cultivated land.

If anyone calls it desecration for small fingers to pull a white horse-gowan, or a blood-red cock-rose, or for a weary wight to sit down on a convenient mossy tombstone above some former wayfarer who needed the staff of life no longer, and munch a mouthful of bread and cheese or bacon, and swallow a draught of milk or beer or cold tea, as the birds pecked the seeds among the grass, and drank the water which gathered in rainy weather in hollows of the road, then Birkenbarns Kirk-yard was desecrated, not otherwise.

But though the kirk-yard gate yielded hospitably to all applicants, the kirk door itself was locked fast from Sunday to Sunday, or as many unyielding Scotch tongues continue to say, with a dogged misappropriation of the Jewish term, from Sabbath to Sabbath. The exceptions were when the minister held his week-day classes or meetings either in the church or the vestry, which was also the session-house. This was a room with whitewashed walls and school-room desk and benches opening from the church. Here were held the meetings of the respectable body of elders—known collectively as the Kirk Session, whose management of parish affairs Bruce had rashly stigmatised; and here the minister was wont to put on and off his Geneva gown, though many an excellent man in hot weather stripped the same from his back in the eyes of the congregation, and hung it without ceremony, like a black flag, over the pulpit railing, preaching in his coat, in which he was fully persuaded his ministrations were as reverent, and his sermon as good and as likely to be profitable to his hearers.

There was not the most distant idea of a daily service at Birkenbarns, or of keeping the church open so that passers-by might enter in and muse and hold their private devotions there. The Scotch mind clings tenaciously to the grand dogma that God is not confined to temples made with hands. Though it has got rid in a great measure of the turbulent independence which tempted it in former centuries to 'ding doon' old cathedrals, and behave with conspicuous, studied indifference more than bordering on irreverence even in its own cherished kirks, and before its own esteemed ministers, just to show that it had no undue superstitious respect for places or persons, it still maintains stoutly that a man can say his prayers as well in his own house or in the fields as in any church. Whether or not the Scotch mind is right in this respect, it is certain that Scotch houses have not become prayerless above all other houses because of this bold conviction. When public halls are not available, the authorities without hesitation grant the kirks for secular, political, philanthropic meetings. The established custom of Iceland has been adopted in cases of need, and the sacred buildings converted into places of shelter for distressed strangers, shipwrecked sailors, even belated holiday makers—ever since the far-back times of civil war when regiments—some of Jacobite, some of Hanoverian troopers—were freely quartered in the parish churches on Saturday night itself. On these occasions remote worshippers coming, without express warning, across the hills and down the meadows for their Sabbath prayers and sermons, found the edifices full of redcoats—men of war who had sometimes the grace to stay—arousing much speculation in the congregations, and listen to the ministers who mounted the pulpit stairs to deliver a message of peace.

Thus it happened that Bruce Kirkpatrick, like the rest of the world, while she sometimes called the church God's house, and was careful of her behaviour there during the service on the Lord's day, attached no particular sanctity to the building at other seasons, when she was as likely to play her pranks there as elsewhere.

It was an unusual event to find the church door ajar, with the key in the lock, on an afternoon, not an evening, and that not on an afternoon answering to the date of one of the minister's meetings. There was not so much as the excuse of organ or choir practising, for there was no organ at Birkenbarns, though the minister, being among the young blood and the new lights in the church, that had seen the world and worshipped in other sanctuaries besides those of their country and nation, had no objection to 'a kist fu o' whistles' in his kirk. As for the choir, it was of the most rustic description, and could never assemble quarter, had been known to render herself a stumbling-block to all the youth present by putting up her parasol in a flood of sunshine, and cocking it in the face of the contumacious blind.

Seeing the minister in his innocent brown study, the spirit of mischief suddenly entered into the gazer. She whisked round to the church door, closed and locked it with a regardless bang and clatter, and when the startled man looked about him in great suprise, and called out, 'Hey! Mathie, I'm not out yet; open the door again,' he was met by a peal of audacious laughter which was certainly not Mathie's. Casting his bewildered eyes out of the window opposite him, they beheld the alarming spectacle of Bruce Kirkpatrick actually skipping to the eminence of the nearest raised flat tomb-stone, brandishing in one hand the ponderous keys of the kirk door, and in the other holding the end of the long rope of the kirk bell which hung in the porch. 'I have you now, Mr. Baillie,' she cried exultingly; 'you did not think me fit for a teacher, and you see what I'm up to. I have locked you into your own church; you are my prisoner at my mercy. If you dare to attempt to scale a wall and escape by a window, I'll toll the bell and summon the whole parish before you have reached the manse.'

Wat hardly doubted that she would keep her word. 'You have taken me by surprise, Miss Bruce,' he tried to say, as quietly as possible. 'How are you? How are your sisters? When do you mean to let me out?' he parleyed with the foe.

'Not till there has been a hue and cry raised on your behalf,' she answered, stamping with her foot to accentuate the rocking motion of the stone, which she seemed to relish. It rested on its pillars unevenly, and swayed from side to side, and she bent herself with the pretty grace and glee of a child to the see-saw. 'I told you what an important person you were, and you pretended not to believe it, while you taunted me with my insignificance. Yes, you did, though of course you did it hypocritically—congratulating me on the dignity of having to wait. You will now have a little of that experience yourself.'

'Don't talk nonsense,' he begged. 'There is no harm in it, and it is amusing in its own way, and at the proper season. But you will understand, if you will reflect for a moment, this is not the place or time, besides I have an engagement this afternoon. Do you hear, Miss Bruce?' he called more imperatively, for he had just remembered with dismay that he had an appointment in less than a quarter of an hour with a labouring man's son, who had contrived to go to college, and what was more to come back with credit. The student desired to put modestly to his predecessor in quitting the ploughshare for the academic hall, the perplexing question, 'What next?' Wat, in spite of his experience, was as much at a loss for an answer as the most of us are in similar circumstances, but all the same he would not fail the lad for the world. It would be too bad if the unjustifiable trick of an idle young lady, even though she happened to be Miss Bruce Kirkpatrick, should detain him beyond his time.

'I wish you to speak sense now,' he urged.

'I don't care,' she replied, with cheerful indifference. 'I don't half believe you. Do reverent ministers ever tell fibs? You did not give me credit for speaking sense.'

He was divided between perplexity and annoyance and a strong sense of the ludicrousness of the situation. He had a remarkably mild temper, and would be the last man to stand on his dignity; still he had an objection to being laughed at and set at nought, in his church too, by a girl eight or ten years his junior. Perhaps it did not lessen the objection that the offender was Miss Bruce Kirkpatrick—the fairy little lady of old. He had not had very much experience in dealing with gay young ladies; altogether he made the mistake of showing he was put out.

'You force me to remind you again, Miss Kirkpatrick, as I have done already, that there is a time for everything. Unfortunately, this afternoon does not suit me for child's play,' he exclaimed, in a vexed, impatient tone.

'Oh, I am a child now,' she caught at the word. 'I thought it would come to that. Do you know, Mr. Baillie, that I was twenty on my last birthday?'

'And do you know,' he prepared to cap her statement, 'I am nearly thirty, and I am your minister, whom you are bound to treat with fitting respect?' he ended, half in jest, half in earnest.

'If you preach another word I'll ring the bell,' she threatened, poising herself with difficulty on the most tottering pinnacle of the stone, so that he was in the liveliest apprehension she might at any instant topple over and come down with a thundering thump, breaking her head like an Irish reaper, or fracturing her arm or spraining her ankle, like a young lady in a novel. In either case what should he do, and how absurdly the story would sound. What would the Misses Kirkpatrick and the brother say? What would the elders and the parish think? If gravity and decorum were to be looked for in any man, it ought to be in a clergyman, whether young or old.

'It will be high time to ring the bell, you know, to summon people to the sermon,' she was explaining, nodding her head in the airiest, most exasperatingly confidential manner. 'I am not going to have another one all to myself, like that I had to listen to coming back from the Bog-o'-mony-stanes.'

'Did you find that so very tiresome?' he asked, in a slightly piqued tone, which was foolish; but the wisest of men have their weaknesses.

'Dreadfully tiresome,' she owned, with perfect candour and coolness.

'What possible motive can you have beyond the purest mischief in keeping me here and forcing me to break my word? I shall be too late for a person who has walked miles to see me.'

'The more fool he! Are you sure it is not she? I beg your pardon, I mean out of church, on a week-day. When you are on the spot you are standing on now, wearing your gown and bands, walking with your hands crossed before you, and your eyes either on the floor or in mid-air looking at nothing, you are entirely master of the situation; but you will allow it is the outsider who has the advantage at the present moment. Mr. Baillie, "honour bright," as Claud used to adjure us, when he was younger and nicer—little boys are so much nicer than big boys—don't you think so? Is there such a person as the one you have alluded to?'

'Of course there is, Miss Bruce,' exclaimed the minister eagerly, with the dawning hope of release. 'What do you take me for?'

'It will do him no harm to wait,' observed Bruce, with gentle meditativeness. 'It is his turn, and he will not be kicking his heels or grinding his teeth. He will be receiving the hospitality of the manse, which Mrs. Baillie will have the opportunity of dispensing to him. They will wonder a little what has become of you, I daresay, but I cannot flatter you by promising their anxiety will spoil their appetites. Besides, the adventure is not like that in the "Mistletoe Bough." This is Thursday;

you will manage to survive two days without food, and a great deal more than your skeleton will be found on Sunday. People are so cold-blooded, and take everything so much for granted nowadays, that they are not likely to send and seek for you.'

'I do not know that,' he muttered under his breath, with a new sense of confusion and annoyance. He would rather almost anything should come to pass than that his mother should arrive on the scene, or even that she should send his father or Rachie and so discover his plight. In many things the Rev. Wat was as ignorant and simple-minded as a baby or as Bruce herself, but he had a more correct idea of the compromising folly of her behaviour. Cæsar's wife was bound to be beyond suspicion —a young lady should be above the merest approach to romping, so should a clergyman. He tried one more remonstrance. 'Miss Bruce, don't be so foolish; we have had enough of this.' He grew severe in the exigency of the circumstances. 'Consider all that would be said if anybody came up and found ——'

'I don't care what people would say; I wish to make a commotion by ringing the church bell, and seeing the people running up panting and staring, thinking the church was on fire. There is nothing save a fire which could happen in this circumscribed sphere. The tower might have been struck by lightning, only we have not had a thunder-storm for weeks. More likely you and Mathie Dobie have been so careless as to leave lucifer matches lying about the session-house, and rats and mice have trodden upon them and set them off. The false alarm would be awfully jolly.' Bruce began to laugh, was in danger of losing her balance, sought to recover it, and, in pulling herself together, jerked the string of the bell and caused it to emit a throttled toll.

'Oh! for Heaven's sake, don't do that!'

cried the minister in despair. 'What do you want? What would you have me to do?'

'I would have you keep from profane swearing,' said Bruce steadily. 'What word was that you uttered just now? You are aware we call that, as you have used it, a bad word in Scotland; and you, a minister! Oh! Mr. Baillie, I am astonished! I am shocked!'

'You would provoke a saint to swear,' he said to himself. He leant back against the window-frame, wiped his forehead, and permitted himself to indulge in a dream of retaliation and revenge.

'If I could catch that lassie, I would give her something to mend her manners, and make her mind what she is about.'

It has been said that the most conspicuous indication of the Rev. Wat's origin, as it still lingered in his bearing, was what is to be found in most self-made men who are thorough gentlemen, in undervaluing their claims and exaggerating their defects, and in remaining at heart as unassuming as when they started in the race of life which has carried them beyond their early contemporaries. There was a shade of stiffness, a degree of elaboration, an approach to old-fashioned stateliness in the young man. But this was only a conscious—the one self-conscious, thing about Wat Baillie, come of his rusticity. Beneath it he was still capable in his manliness and goodness of breaking out and expressing himself, both by word and act, in a primitive manner, which, however transparently innocent, would have better become a peasant than a peer let us say. There are nature's gentlemen everywhere; but it takes three generations, so the world reckons, to make a conventional gentleman.

He sought to defy her, as he ought to have done in the beginning. 'I don't care, Miss Bruce, according to your favourite declaration;

do you hear? I am going to take a nap in the pulpit.'

'It is no more than your due, after all the naps we have had in the seats. But you ought to have a lulling voice in your ears to send you over sweetly to the land of dreams. Shall I say something? I mean, shall I repeat some of my old schoolroom recitations?'

'No, thanks; you need not trouble to wait any longer. You'll miss something or other— your afternoon tea. I shall not miss mine particularly, since I had a good dinner. I shall be all the hungrier for the next meal, after I have been traced. Don't wait; good-bye. On second thoughts I shall not take a nap, but compose my next week's sermon, and put into it ——'

'I'll ring the bell!'

'Do. Let us have it all—the entire programme. The tired people in the fields and cottages will be frightened out of their wits.

Weary already with their day's work, they will weary themselves still further by hurrying here, to find they have been taken in and made game of by an idle young lady.'

The permission was a dangerous experiment, but it answered his purpose. She did not accept it. 'You don't send me to the manse to tell them why you have not returned,' she remarked, in a more forced manner, as if the joke were beginning to pall and fall to pieces.

'No, don't trouble yourself,' he pursued his advantage; 'I was only going to say that I have given in. I am in your power to make me look like a fool without any fault of mine, or else—but I prefer the first alternative, to cause me to appear to act with discourtesy and unkindness to a good fellow—as good as myself—very likely a great deal better. Miss Bruce, don't abuse your power, when I ask it as a favour if you will put back the key in the door, turn the lock, and let me out.'

'Why did you not say that before?' demanded Bruce, in an aggrieved tone, leaping down from her tombstone, walking straight to the door, opening it, and holding out her hand. 'Will you shake hands with me after what I've done? Will you ever forgive me? I hope I have not really inconvenienced you. It was very wild and thoughtless of me, but you see I am a good deal sat upon—one way and another,' she said the words with a struggling sigh. 'Though Mary and Lily are the kindest souls breathing, and poor Claud cannot altogether help being out of joint—as the whole world is some people say, I do not often get my head out. You are not very angry at a stupid piece of fun?'

'No, no; don't mention it,' he assured her, more abashed by her penitence than by her raillery, while she looked up with her fearless bright brown eyes in his face. 'I am glad you have such fine spirits, only you will allow me to say you should keep them under control, when they interfere——'

'With the freedom of the subject.' She took the word out of his mouth, with a return of roguishness in her eyes and speech, 'especially the ministerial subject. But I do respect my minister, if you will believe me, Mr. Baillie; I meant no offence, as poor people say.'

'Well, no offence is taken; you may see that,' he said, with a little gruffness, to hide some other feeling, as he took the hand held out to him. 'You are all well at Birkencraig? Miss Lily does not suffer from the east wind?' forgetting that he had asked for both sisters long before.

But after he had parted from Bruce at the churchyard gate in a perfectly matter-of-fact manner, he said to himself in a tone of foreboding, as he strode towards the manse, making up for lost time, 'That poor lassie will get herself and somebody else into a bad scrape before she has done.'

CHAPTER IX.

THE RED-CROSS AMBULANCE CLASS.

Bruce Kirkpatrick did not meet the minister of Birkenbarns again, out of church, unless in the most cursory way, until spring had passed into summer, summer into autumn, and the heat of harvest was over. As far as they knew, nobody except themselves was acquainted with her escapade on the spring afternoon. It would be hard to say whether or not the recollection never returned to them out of season, in the very scene of the poor little joke; whether, when her eyes chanced to glance out of a particular window and fall on a certain flat tombstone, the corners of her mouth did not curl ever so slightly, and she would put down her head and occupy herself with her book. It might be that he was moved by the sense of a secret between them, however trifling, while he was quick to follow her glance, interpret her expression, and even respond to it with a fleeting twinkle of his grey eyes.

Good people have been considerably exercised by the relation or non-relation between humour and godliness; whether the two qualities can be coexistent, and whether the first will survive in a higher sphere. Surely whatever is purely human comes near to the divine. The perpetual union of pathos with humour shows its grand capabilities. A passing reflection of mirth, a momentary realisation of the quaint and grotesque in the most serious mind, can no more disturb a healthy humble awe and reverence and hearty piety, than a child's crow will introduce a jarring discord into a grandsire's prayer. Wat Baillie was filled with his message, and was as loyally, blissfully in earnest as man could be. It has been before mentioned that Bruce Kirkpatrick, however foolish, would no more have coquetted and played herself during the public worship of God than she would have coquetted and played herself on her death-bed, knowing it to be her death-bed. She was in earnest in her own way, and a model of seriousness and sobriety sometimes. She was not only on her best behaviour in church on Sundays, she liked to listen to Wat Baillie's sermons, and desired to be the better for them, though she never dilated on them in a style of general inflated worthless eulogium such as Mary and Lily, with the most of the church-going old women in the parish, indulged in.

But Bruce retained a little of the soreness on the score of spiritual and mental inferiority with which the Rev. Wat had contrived unwittingly to inspire her. She knew she was idle, discontented, and often ill-tempered, while uncouth, plodding Rachie Baillie was industrious, satisfied, and serene. Bruce was keenly conscious that she was far behind the minister and his sister in intellectual acquirements. The youngest Miss Kirkpatrick was as badly educated as young ladies mostly are. She did not so much as know the names of some of those ancient and modern philosophers —'wise, auld billies like Plato and Socrates, Aristotle and Epicurus,' or 'gergan, long-headed, teuch chaps like Kant and Hegel,' as Rachie had appreciatively defined them, when the wind of some engrossing discussion with her brother had blown them into Bruce Kirkpatrick's ears, and these had been tickled by faint echoes of systems profound, speculative, practical, and mystical, with which she could no more cope than she could expound the Differential Calculus. History remained the shreds and patches of dry and barren lessons to Bruce, while to

Wat and Rachie it was the mighty-sounding yet beautifully minute and perfect course of God's providence among the nations, which now roared and spouted like great sea billows, now dropped softly and noiselessly like pearls of dew. In poetry and imaginative literature Bruce felt herself nearly as much humbled. She was quite capable of liking melodious lyrics and songs and enjoying good novels, but what was that tiny advance, which merely carried her a step beyond the region of the intelligent Scotch cook and dairymaid, when Wat and Rachie not only did as much and a great deal more in that department, they actually relished epic poems, and counted it the richest treat to read a play of Shakespeare which they had never seen played?

If Bruce had but guessed it, there was a grain of grace and hope in this sense of her shortcomings; but alas! in addition to the mortification and depression which they caused her, she had no reason to cherish the slightest expectation of ever correcting them in kind; she was well aware she had not a particle of intellectual taste beyond the point given. No Kirkpatrick that she had heard of ever dreamt of being a scholar. Scholarship was not in her race. So Bruce, secretly smarting at the lack of the very inclination for it, took to decrying it, and making satirical speeches about bookworms and blue-stockings, which were wasted on Mary and Lily.

One may easily comprehend the eagerness and exultation with which Bruce welcomed a new field of enterprise, and entered on it, conscious that she could not only hold her own and win laurels in it, but prove that there was a line in which no Baillie could approach her.

As a valuable legacy left by the last wars in Europe and America, and a fresh, if somewhat fantastic, development of the ancient order of St. John of Jerusalem, ambulance classes had suddenly sprung up in the large towns, and were well attended. Doctors and medical students delivered lectures on the best and quickest way of dealing with the victims of accidents in the fields and workshops, and with the sufferers from domestic disasters, so that fellow-workers, ordinary bystanders, and the simple women of a household might give valuable help before trained professional aid could be procured. Thus the minimum of pain and death might be attained.

Wat Baillie's attention was particularly called to the subject by an unwonted number of casualties which happened in the harvest field this year. A reaper bled to death from the incapacity of anybody round her to form a tourniquet and stop the flow of life-blood from the severed artery. A bandster, who was 'auld and wrunkled and grey,' became insensible from heat and fatigue, and was allowed to pass away in his swoon because no one near him knew how to recover a man from a fainting-fit. There were other unfortunate occurrences—falls, and an involuntary plunge into the Bog Burn, which did not prove fatal, but had almost done so, and would certainly have inflicted far less injury had the commonest acquaintance with physical laws and with the most easily obtained remedies been general

The Rev. Wat entered on the question with characteristic zeal and enthusiasm. He fee'd and coaxed the young country doctor, who was not his Elder—the older doctor was not a big enough man to be open to such a revolutionary movement. The junior medical man came across to Birkenbarns on two evenings in the week to teach the rudiments of the art of healing to a heterogeneous class assembled for the purpose of receiving useful information of a vital kind in the manse dining-room, made to serve as an improvised schoolroom.

The minister delivered only one lecture in

the series. He explained that the days of old hereditary nostrums, with a few precious elements of truth in them, and the ready resource derived from sheer mother wit, were passing away. We had changed all that. A partial education had swept aside and was even tending to paralyse the capabilities of shrewd ignorance left to its own devices. The time for greater knowledge—the knowledge of schools, had come everywhere. Then he told what an ambulance meant, and what was the origin of the term Red Cross in connection with it. He soothed the jealous susceptibilities of the more thoughtful among the audience lest the words should refer to anything popish, while he gave an account of the ancient order of St. John of Jerusalem, and sought to illustrate the manner in which the solacing of the unfortunate and miserable had always blended with the practice of true religion. After his part was played, the Rev. Wat left the desk with the greatest alacrity and installed himself as the first pupil in the class. He induced Rachie, in spite of her shyness, to make the second. There followed a tolerable gathering of the more intelligent and docile of the ploughmen and craftsmen accustomed to appear in the minister's young men's class. These aspirants to knowledge gaped and grinned and felt tempted to nudge each other at the marvels of the map of a skeleton, another map of veins and arteries, a piece of dried skin, a bit of crumbling bone. A second Elder, the riddle-maker, was there, partly with a worthy desire to support his minister, partly with an unquenchable craving, which Wat had to resist, to change the subject of the lecture and put in a word for the soul when it was the body which was being discussed.

The greatest difficulty had been found in bringing out a few homely mothers of families, either belonging to, or just above, the class that attended Rachie's mothers' meetings. These naïve women showed that they regarded it as a very different thing to consent to Rachie Baillie's request to work for an hour under her competent directions, receiving the petticoat or jacket they had made as a reward for their exertions, and to be so forward and wanting in proper feeling—though it was their minister who bade them—as to go to the manse and sit alongside of gentlemen and some of the men of their own households, hearkening to a young doctor discoursing on matters which approached perilously near to 'people's insides.' Men and women, aye, and bairns, died by quiet or violent deaths, when it was the Lord's will and their time had come. Sickness was bad enough to 'thole' when it was among them, without their going half-way to meet it. There was a mixture of fatalistic doctrine and false humility in these women which made it exasperating to deal with them. In spite of the constant danger of their being brought into close contact with cuts, bruises, and burns, the wives and mothers would not admit that these 'troubles,' in which so much was dependent on the women's presence of mind and skill, belonged to their province. They took little interest in what might have been the familiar topics. Notwithstanding the laboured simplicity of the language and examples which were used, the members of this section of the audience were constantly dropping off to sleep, or finding themselves under the necessity of immediately returning home at the crisis of the lesson. Wat had to speak a word for the reluctant scholars when the doctor would have lost patience altogether. 'They are so unaccustomed to sit with their hands still, poor bodies! I wonder if it could be managed for them to bring a bit of knitting or sewing. No? You think that would distract their minds still farther. They are so unused to the painful operation of thinking, that even its earliest beginning in careful observation is a tiresome task for them.'

There were one or two older women who were more promising scholars, when sufficient allowance was made for the fact that they were decidedly opinionative, disposed to be sceptical and to believe that they knew a great deal better on almost every count. For they held the doctor to be a mere babe, in experience as well as in years, in comparison with any one of themselves. They had already a large proportion of the medical practice of their class in the parish in their hands. Being, as it were, doctors without diplomas, they brought a considerable acquaintance with outward symptoms and an inevitable interest in them to bear on the lecture. Wat considered it quite a diplomatic stratagem and triumph to have got the patronage and countenance of the disengaged of these elderly ladies for his class.

Bruce Kirkpatrick excited a sensation when, brimming over with youth, grace, pleasant excitement, and fearless enterprise, she joined the class. 'I think I can learn something here. I have not two left hands, though I am almost afraid I have two left brains for dry, heavy books. I am not frightened—none of us is easily frightened, except Mary—for carriage accidents. I have persuaded my sisters to let me come; I did not mind Claud. I would not hear of being kept away.'

In truth, Miss Kirkpatrick and Miss Lily had not been very willing that Bruce should be taught to 'dress wounds,' as they defined the object of the class, even at the instigation of the minister. In spite of their kindness and gentleness, the sisters were among the old-fashioned people who still 'go in' for the ignorance and helplessness of ladies, with the reservation of a few strictly stereotyped performances. Young ladies especially ought to know nothing more than graces and accomplishments, with a superficially scanty crop of the last. Beyond this, Claud might give Bruce a few additional lessons in driving, at the imminent risk of breaking her neck; or if she chose to shoot with his lightest pistol in the gallery or at the target in the park, she would always be bearing her brother company. The sisters, particularly Lily, would not quite like Bruce to progress till she shot pigeons and rabbits with her own hand, but fishing was a pretty sport for a lady. Fish were not like beasts, they gave one the idea of being unfeeling somehow, so that nobody thought anything of the cold-blooded pangs of a trout. Even if the minister were very anxious for the young sister to take a class—the class of the tidiest, best-behaved girls, now and then, by way of example, in the Sabbath school, it could not be called a desirable proceeding, still it was permissible, and a point might be stretched. But what call had Bruce to go and look at wounds, and dress them? The bare idea was horrible, absolutely revolting, though the whole General Assembly thought fit to endorse it. The ladies must have held, without any examination, the parable of 'The Good Samaritan' to be local or purely figurative in its application. If the Misses Kirkpatrick did not go so far as to think it 'rude' and 'not good for a girl' to hear and speak of her 'inside,' or indeed of any other part of her body which was not discussed in a dressmaker's sense, they regarded such discussion as unfit for Bruce, who was too independent in her notions already.

But Bruce had her will, as she usually got it with her sisters, and presented herself radiant at the class. This was the greater feat on her part, since the woman who was the *bête noire* of the elder Misses Kirkpatrick's imaginations, she who represented to them, as to many men on whose favour the former belles of Birkencraig set exaggerated store, the most degraded and offensive of her sex, was that product of modern times, styled by these old-fashioned judges, with unnecessary repetition of the feminine gender, 'a lady-doctoress.' They could find pity for a poor fallen creature, who had been deluded and dragged down into sin and shame, but for a brazen-faced aspirant to the honours and privileges, nay, to the very duties of men, the ladies had no excuse.

The most dissentient voice, after the voices of the Misses Kirkpatrick, on the ambulance question was Mrs. Baillie's. She considered Wat going out of his way and demeaning himself by taking up a doctor's 'trade,' though she herself would have prescribed and administered without hesitation to any unfortunate applicant some of the deadliest drugs in the pharmacopœia. The 'lowdamy' (laudanum) and 'calamy' (calomel) quoted to Sir Walter Scott by a self-taught Scotch medicine man, have not vanished from the medicine shelves of the lower middle classes, any more than the sulphur and treacle of Dotheboys Hall. For Miss Bruce Kirkpatrick the pretence at learning 'to doctor' was vain show. For Rachie, whose brains were muddled with book-learning, whose great fingers wavered and 'bogled,' and never went skilfully about anything, save the use of her needle and shears, for which she had to thank her mother and a long apprenticeship to a 'purpose' particular dressmaker, Mrs. Baillie would not like to be the man or woman whom Rachie would take it upon her to nurse. For the deluded working women whom Wat had decoyed into wasting so much of their time on two evenings of the week at the manse—set them up! some of the silly creatures were not fit for anything, but they knew as much as their mothers knew before them, as any 'working-man's' wife needed to know—if they could 'festen a leech' and make a bit 'trate-claith' (a mysterious Scotch preparation of calico, beeswax and lard, long devoutly believed in and applied as a sovereign remedy for every description of hurt). The sole result of Wat's experiment which Mrs. Baillie looked for, was the amount of clay that some of the scholars brought in on their hob-nailed shoes and diligently scraped off on the dining-room carpet. Well for the manse if that had been all the harm done.

Wat had thought to stimulate his fellow-pupils by offering a few prizes for competition, mostly simple books on animal physiology. He hoped these would be won by his most sensible lads, or, what would be next best, by one or other of the wise elderly women, as rewards for attainments in answering questions, writing down the plainest summary—eccentric grammar and phonetic spelling not proving a barrier to success—showing how a poultice should be made and a bandage put on. But, somewhat to his disturbance, the lion's share of the prizes was gained by Bruce Kirkpatrick. She was so alert and neat-handed, with a certain native force and fineness of discrimination and execution, lightness and tenderness of touch. What wretched bunglers he and Rachie were beside her! How far even the longest-headed, most highly-experienced of the elderly ladies who came nearest the successful competitor, fell behind her. How the doctor warmed to his apt pupil, and praised her achievements enthusiastically. As he was not the Kirkpatricks' doctor, was a married man, and was, as one of the few liberals in the district, even snobbish in his democratic scorn of the aristocracy, represented by the small crop of lairds' families, he might be reckoned singularly impartial. What a treat it would be to have such a nurse in sickness instead of Mrs. Baillie or even Rachie! How freely a man might consent to be ill, to find himself so well and daintily dealt with in his progress to recovery!

Bruce was as proud as a child of both prizes and commendations. They showed she had been right in judging herself not utterly incapable. She did not care though Claud derided her gains, and even Mary and Lily, for a wonder, looked slightingly on them. But she had quieted her sisters' fears by not proposing to make any immediate personal use of her acquirements in dressing wounds. She had only once, and that was not in her sisters' presence, startled the doctor and Wat, and set them thinking, by abruptly asking, when the three happened to be alone together, whether concussion of the brain or internal injuries occurred oftenest in carriage accidents, and what had better be done when people talked a great deal, started and trembled in their sleep.

One natural consequence of Bruce's attendance at the ambulance class was that she became on much more familiar terms with the manse family, especially with the minister and

Rachie. The brother and sister, of course, approached a great deal nearer Bruce in position than her other class-fellows, and a comparative intimacy had sprung up between the three—inadvertently enough—but promising to be permanently established. Bruce said to herself and her family, she was bound in common gratitude to remember the benefit she had derived from the lessons she had shared with the ploughmen and old wives. She did not cease to call frequently at the manse, after the class had come to an end, and to receive an increasing amount of satisfaction and interest from the intercourse—a boon in Bruce's drowsy, poverty-stricken, terror-crossed life. It was at the height of the pheasant shooting. Claud was enough engaged not to want much from the women, even to forget to notice and find fault with Bruce's doings. As for Miss Kirkpatrick and Miss Lily, if Claud were pleased, or not too violently displeased, they let Bruce do very much as she liked.

The October weather was fine and mellow, an English version of an Indian summer in the crisp, frosty, broadly diffused sunshine over the bare stubble and yellowing turnip-fields. There was still a wealth of berries beginning to be tinted everywhere with the richest, subtlest dyes. The very humble wayside weeds, the silver-weed and the dock, vied with each other in amber, and crimson, and bronze. The manse garden was glorious—from its scarlet-streaked russet apples, the fast-perishing foliage of its cherry-trees, and the sunny splendour of its dahlias and hollyhocks—down to the exquisite variety of colour in the feathery leaves in its carrot beds. The Craig above stood out ruddy still, with lingering, unfaded heather against the blue sky.

Bruce came generally just before the daylight departed, as she was returning from some walk for which she had lost her afternoon tea, and found the minister and Rachie, after their tea, loitering for the quarter of an hour of blindman's holiday in the gloaming garden.

The minister was not only bound, he was ready, to welcome any of his parishioners. To add that he was heartily glad to see this one— who had been capable of behaving like a naughty, heedless child, whom old Nanny at the Toll, and many more than Nanny, pronounced to be still destitute of grace, who was full of faults—is only to allow that he was a man and a young man.

Rachie was more dubious in the light in which she viewed Bruce Kirkpatrick's visits. Rachie rather liked Bruce after the two had became better acquainted, though the young lady was always laughing—perhaps to hide a sore heart, the minister warned his sister—but on the whole Bruce hurt the *ci-devant* dressmaker less than most ladies hurt her. It was not that Bruce Kirkpatrick was without family pride, but she thought too little of herself and her circumstances to show herself affable and condescending in her frank friendliness towards Rachie. Still the self-consciousness of the latter came between them, and bred jealousy of her new associate. Rachie was especially distrustful of Bruce's bearing to the minister. Rachie, with her woman's intuition, was forced to suspect that Miss Bruce laughed at, as well as with, Wat, and that offence was simply unpardonable. Rachie had a great enough heart and soul to condone most injuries to herself, but she could not look over a flippant liberty taken with Wat, a careless slight to him—a scholar, who had lived among gentlemen as their equal; a licensed, ordained minister—the gibing lassie's own minister. That Wat should be blind or magnanimous to the deepest shade of the enormity only rendered it more heinous in Rachie's faithful eyes.

Late one afternoon the three friends were in the garden, as near the foot as the strawberry beds, in which the leaves were curling up, shrivelling and falling off straw-coloured, brown and ashen-hued, with a faint delicate odour.

Bruce had already called upon the minister to climb a tree and pull a special apple she coveted. Her host and squire for the moment had obeyed her behest, unsuited as his rather ponderous figure and clerical costume were for the undertaking. To her secret amusement and slight consternation, which Rachie somehow guessed, he had gone through the unexpected preparation of deliberately pulling off his coat and appearing in his shirt sleeves. After all, the costume, though it was not *de rigueur*, might be regarded as decorous in essentials as cricket or boating flannels. It might be worn in exceptional circumstances; it has been adopted with advantage under press of climate, in full dress by a high official—one of the wisest and best of governors-general. We have it on the excellent authority of a bright, cheery eye-witness, that the governor-general of an important group of South Sea Islands appeared with the gentlemen of his suite at dinner in government house in their shirt sleeves. We are also told that with the fine touches of crimson silk sashes and embroidered braces the costume would be highly becoming. Wat had laid aside his hat also, and then had proceeded slowly to climb the tree, with his face lifted up and his eyes fixed on the goal of his enterprise. His projecting ears were thus conspicuous, and aroused a new simile in Bruce's prodigal mind. 'How like an ourang-outang you look up there in the tree, Mr. Baillie,' she called to him. That saucily impertinent comparison and a single easily said word of thanks were all he had for his trouble, and he seemed to think them enough too!

The next flight of Bruce's nimble fancy was that she saw a fish's scales glisten under a stone in the little garden burn. She tempted Wat to descend the bank to the edge of the shallow water, the better to reconnoitre, when his foot slipped and he went splashing into the stony channel llike an over-grown school-boy wading to catch minnows. Domestic and harmless as the burn was, it had some tolerably deep holes, as the minister knew, and if he stumbled into one of them he might have cause to regret—though he remained destitute of his coat—that he was not in other respects in the light rig of a wader or shrimper. He stooped down to feel the ground, and suddenly and sharply withdrew his hand.

Rachie gaped like the ploughboys in the class, and Bruce's bright colour fled in an instant.

'Is it an adder?' she cried, with bated breath. 'Oh, don't say it is an adder. Do they come here? Do they take to the water? Oh, I am so sorry I did not ask the doctor what to put to an adder's bite. It was very silly of me; but I was afraid you would all laugh at me.'

'I should just say so. Why, Miss Bruce, you are a complete victim to adder-phobia. Somebody will play a trick on you if you do not take care, since it is so well known you are beyond the pale of reason where " laidly worms " are concerned. Adders, indeed! I should have been better off in a nest of adders. I say, Rachie, somebody before our day must have been in the habit of flinging broken glass amongst the stones of the burn. Look here, you two surgeresses,' and he held out a broad wrist, across which there was a long cut, from which blood was flowing freely.

Alas! for Rachie's presence of mind, self-control, and the power of behaving with the greatest judiciousness which her recent studies should have taught her, the first time these invaluable qualifications were called into action. She grew very faint and sick when she saw a real wound—Wat's blood flowing in this alarming fashion—as if she had never heard of a tourniquet or handled a bandage. She might have fallen into the burn next if she had not instinctively obeyed Bruce's imperative indignant order: 'Sit down, Miss Baillie; sit down this moment. Hold down you head as the doctor told you to do. Don't stir till you feel yourself getting red in the face, or I shall have you fainting on my hands, when you know I ought to be binding up the minister's wrist.'

For the moment Bruce was as grave as a judge, while it was Wat's turn to laugh and rally her a little on the excellent opportunity for exercising her skill. He was tempted to think she had planned the whole affair—bit of glass included—and sent him down to the burn as the destined patient.

Bruce bravely put her fingers on what might be a severed artery and held the wound closed, while she bade him give her his handkerchief. The handkerchief was not to be had on the instant; it was in the pocket of his coat lying beneath the apple-tree, while her handkerchief was too small and slight in texture. She marched him away, a willing captive, with her dabbled hand pressing his wrist, as if to count the pulse-beats that sent the blood welling to her finger-tips, leaving Rachie sitting holding down her head obediently among the strawberry beds.

It was only after Bruce had really, with considerable spirit and dexterity, dressed a wound, bound it up, with every chance of staunching the blood and preventing any farther harm, and removed all traces of the accident, that the demon of mischief returned and took possession of her. She began in her innocent girlish folly to torment her Samson. She told him to hold his hand this way and that way. She threatened him with the most terrible consequences if he did not submit to her authority. She dared him to depart from a regimen on which she would at once put him. He was not to swallow a mouthful of supper beyond a glass of claret and a biscuit. He was to go to bed at ten o'clock sharp. He was to sleep for a round of the clock. He was to be very careful what he ate for breakfast, and then—well, she would tell him what then when she called the first thing in her round of visits next morning.

> 'He laughed a laugh of merry scorn;
> He turned and kissed her where she stood.'

Alas! still more for Wat than for Rachie, but he was a man before he was a minister. He had been a homely young countryman who had seen wild girls punished in the fashion the most unsophisticated, which came most readily to hand, long before he was a conventional gentleman. No man breathing was more incapable of a real insult or even a small unkindness to a woman than Wat Baillie, but it might well be that on provocation he forgot his elaborate politeness, and returned to the rude simplicity of his youth. Perhaps—for the fate of two lives seems sometimes to hang on a straw—the want of his coat without the excuse of the tropical climate, or the compensating picturesqueness of the crimson sash, recalled the undress of a carter and old associations too powerfully. Perhaps Bruce's serge gown, with the light shawl crossed in front and knotted behind, as a child, or a graceful young girl would wear it, and the somewhat weather-beaten Rubens hat, were not enough to turn the scales. An excellent woman who dressed superbly, and delivered religious addresses at meetings of working men, gave as a reason for the costly and tasteful dress at which some stupid censor was carping enough to cavil, that she wore it in order to please her masons, and make her bakers and butchers respect her. Bruce might have pleased Wat Baillie without securing his respect. For the last achievement the flashing diamonds, cobweb lace, and long trailing pale blue and pink silk gowns, worn on a summer afternoon, in a country garden, by a modern American young lady, might have been absolutely necessary, though most reflective people would have argued the very reverse.

If it was the lack of his coat that was in fault, the effect was similar to the fatal spell of 'them boots' which walked of their own accord into all the alehouses, carrying with them all the poor pauper women who wore the possessed articles of dress in their erratic yet methodical course.

'How dare you, Mr. Baillie!' cried Bruce,

with her face all on fire, retreating several paces. Then she had an inkling of the swift retribution which had come upon him in his immediate discomfiture and distress. The extreme ludicrousness of the situation got the better of her, as on a former occasion, and she began to laugh. 'I will tell your Elders. I will bring it before the Presbytery. You'll be suspended. You'll lose your church.'

When it came to that there was more genuine refinement in Wat Baillie than in Bruce Kirkpatrick. Here was he scarlet with confusion and vexation, and fit to slay himself with self-reproach for the rash impulse of a moment which had caused him to forget his cloth, and, what was worse, her trust in him and the cordiality and kindness which had placed her in his power. He had wounded her pride and delicate high spirit in all her antecedents; he had affronted her in her young ladyhood. A girl like Rachie would have been justly angry with a young man who had taken a mean advantage of a girl's fun and nonsense, and would have shaken him off roughly, perhaps; but she need not have minded so much. This was altogether different. Miss Bruce Kirkpatrick had been the little lady of his hobbledehoyhood, and he was her minister. He could have gone down on his knees to beg her pardon—an abasement which would only have afforded her further diversion; for she was able to laugh in his face, to laugh the matter off—even to make stock of it for further teasing, supposing they should still continue to be on intimate terms.

Truly this capacity on Bruce's part administered something like an additional shock to the poor minister in the middle of his contrition. Such a freely-snatched kiss would have appeared a commoner, more natural occurrence to his sister, yet Rachie might have 'thought shame' to speak of it afterwards.

There was a strain of levity and coarseness in the Kirkpatrick women, possibly contracted unawares from their association with the ignoble men of the race. Such a strain may be present in many a fine lady whose manners are unexceptionable, and absent in many a peasant woman whose manners are below par. It had been evident in both Mary and Lily Kirkpatrick in their day. Once, long ago, Mary had chanced to enter on a flirtation with one of her many admirers in so unsuitable a place for such a private gratification as the most frequented shop in Sauchope. The lady had got so much into the spirit of the play, and had actually enjoyed the publicity of the performance to such a degree, that she carried it on for three mortal hours, until nine-tenths of the better class gossips in the town entered the shop on one pretence and another, to witness and comment on the scandal. At last the autocratic laird discovered what his daughter was about, made his appearance on the scene, too much incensed to hide his wrath, ordered her away as if they were people of quite low extraction, and, it was said, prohibited Miss Kirkpatrick from putting a foot in the streets of Sauchope for the next six months.

It was on the cards that Bruce might not be above deriving some poor pleasure from the minister's getting into a little trouble on her account. But then the trouble must not be great; and even in that light it was because Bruce was an ignorant as well as an ill-brought-up girl, ignorant of much trouble and misery, that she could contemplate even a little with equanimity, nay, with selfish gratification, as a tribute to her power.

Bruce composed herself presently, and went away as if nothing had happened.

It was the minister who was thoroughly discomfited and unhappy. But even he failed to distinguish a certain ominously appropriate merriment in the kitchen where the servant had a visitor, which called forth more than one angry remark from Mrs. Baillie, and at last brought down a severe rebuke on the culprit when she was at a signal disadvantage, since she had been summoned to prayers, and was therefore before the assembled family as before a public tribunal.

'What's a' that keechlin' about, Sairey? Unco-like on-goings in a manse kitchen. I will not have them. I will not allow you to have company if this is to be the upshot.'

Even if Wat had not been conscience-stricken, he must have hastened to give out the psalm in order to release the prisoner caught in a trap. He did not understand, any more than the others, the exact meaning of the pursing up of Sairey's mouth and the carriage of her head as she sat down near the door, without a spoken word of self-defence, and proceeded to seek out the verse and sing in a shrill treble. The silent protest was as follows: 'Carry on, mistress. What's to hinder you? But you'll maybe hear mair o' the on-goings this e'enin', Mistress Beelyie—a hantle mair than you'll like, before a's done; though I dinna want to wacht the minister, puir frail man. Ye had better look to the ha' company as well as to the puir folk in the kitchen, though I trow you're mair acquent wi' the last. Ye'll better keep a ticht hand on your ain bairns and the very minister himsel'. I'm muckle obleeged to you, I'm sure, Mrs. Beelyie mem, but let charity begin at hame.'

CHAPTER X.

'HAMESUCKEN.'

'So, Claud, my fine fellow, you are likely to have a parson for a brother-in-law. He will " dress" you, as the natives say. A parson in one's family circle is no joke. I know something of it, though I make myself rather scarce at the Marquis's hearth since Lady Elizabeth married the Archdeacon' (Lord Sandy always gave the members of his family their full titles when he spoke of them to his associates). 'But to have a regular John Knox, and a clodhopper to boot—if you will forgive me for saying so just this once, Kirkpatrick—all to yourself, is an awful dispensation. By Jove, he will pitch into you, hot and strong. I should not like to be you, my boy. You will become a pattern of all the virtues when the minister takes you in hand.'

The speaker was Lord Sandy, seeking, for lack of better amusement, to tease Claud Kirkpatrick, as this promising scion of the aristocracy would tease his bull-dog, to the verge of madness.

The place was a private room in the Royal Albert Hotel, Sauchope, where the young men had been playing cards, and having a pipe and something to drink on a stormy October afternoon. Claud Kirkpatrick was sitting flushed and in a heady state like the liquor, hovering between overpowering boisterousness, dire quarrelsomeness, and flat stupor.

The only other person present was one of the horse-dealers, whose company was so much affected by the young laird. He was a low type of man, with a bull-neck and small forehead, a red nose, the high colour of which was partly due to exposure to the weather, but was indebted also to the fact that its possessor stopped his trap at every ale-house of every road he drove on. As a suitable adjunct to the nose there were pairs of ferrety eyes and thick turned-over lips. The man was a good deal of a brute by nature and more brutified by training and habit; still he was not of the decidedly blackguard order of Lord Sandy, with his hook nose, hollow, half-burnt-out eyes, lantern jaws, and long chin.

Claud had been soaking his wits, far from bright at the best, and he did not at first take up the allusion.

'I don't know what you're driving at, you sarcastic beggar,' he said, with the amiable sulkiness which was chronic with him.

'What, are you the last to be told? Come, this is too bad, and you the head of the house, when the whole parish is ringing with the news. Perhaps your friends think you'll know soon enough, as people do when a bank fails, or your nearest relative proposes to remove you to a lunatic asylum. It is not a bad move on the old girls' part from their point of view, and bonnie Bruce, though she is a spitfire, is sacrificing herself in the most approved sisterly fashion.'

Claud sat dumb, positively choking with bewilderment and rage.

'By George! it's another grand lift for the minister,' said the horse-dealer hastily. He desired to calm down a gathering tempest by the first word of flattery he could find for his patron. 'I mind well before Tammas Bilie was grieve at Rintoul, when he wrocht a pair of horses on the farm. It is a fine thing to have brains and study divinity, and get first the kirk and then the leddy-wife with her influential kindred to hold up his dignity.'

Claud had recovered his speech by this time; but he used such ugly words, that he would have been as well, and better, without the gift for the present. The substance of his vehement protest was still, What did they mean? Whom were they calling 'old girls,' 'bonnie Bruces,' and 'spitfires'? He was determined to know, though the knowledge might not be to the benefit of some of the speakers, who were taking beastly liberties. It was a big lie—the most insolent and groundless of lies, which he would cast in the teeth of any man who should dare to repeat it.

In his downward course Lord Sandy had been forced to rub shoulders with a good many indignities, and to put up with them superciliously and doggedly. But he had not yet accepted the lie direct from Claud Kirkpatrick, whose limited sense forsook him entirely when he had taken an enemy into his mouth to steal away his brains, and was besides distraught with passion. He then showed a peculiar development, which was a mixture of the savage and the idiot.

Lord Sandy did not catch up his riding-whip, with which he was usually armed, and lay it across Claud's slouched shoulders on the spot. Neither did the insulted man throw his glass in his neighbour's face, and grind his teeth— perhaps because he had few left to grind, though he bared those few fangs in a vicious grin, while his swarthy complexion darkened to a purplish hue. 'Look here, Kirkpatrick,' he recommended the younger man with exasperating composure, 'if you will be a fool, make a row, and stand the consequences, take care you have it out in the right quarter. Don't go and quarrel with your friends, man. Ask the precious peeping beadle of your blessed kirk and the curious jade of a manse servant what delicious morsel of tittle-tattle they have been spreading about for the last fortnight, till the whole neighbourhood is on the *qui vive*, laughing in its sleeve, ready to explode in a horse-laugh at any moment. I can tell you something else than an insult and an assault is due to a good-natured sinner, who is ready to look over your cursed temper and put you on your guard. Miss Bruce would not have a word to say to a ne'er do-well like me, hang it! but the demure little devil—pardon me once more, for a single moment, my boy— you know women will be women all alike, though they hail from the same quarter as ourselves—Miss Bruce could lay aside her decorum to the extent of playing tricks on the great hulking minister-fellow, locking him up in his church, when these two must have been carrying on a Scotch wooing in the churchyard of all places. Then there was the farce of the sawbones class; till at last the woman—the maid-servant, watched her master privileged to take a kiss from the young lady in the open garden, in enough daylight to be spied upon from the kitchen or the dairy window. I appeal to you, is it not time that the marriage should be announced, or at least that you should be made aware of the honour awaiting you in the intended family arrangement?'

Claud was held at bay, but he remained furiously incredulous. One of his idiosyncrasies was an almost insane idea of the social importance of the family which he was dragging down by his mental and moral inferiority and constant misconduct. He had been provoked with Bruce for her alliance with the manse from the date of the ambulance class, but he had never degraded her, in his imagination, by the most distant suspicion of philandering with Muckle Wat. Claud Kirkpatrick in his clownishness and scampishness would as soon have supposed that his young sister could consent to flirt with Nicol the butler, if he had been a young man, as with any minister, doctor, writer (lawyer), or banker between Birkencraig and Edinburgh. The last were very different persons, but Claud chose to lump them together. Of course, a marriage with the parish minister, Tammas Baillie of Rintoul's son, was not to be thought of for an instant for one of the Misses Kirkpatrick.

It was an idle, base fabrication, Claud said, in a good deal stronger language than is preserved here. But he cried out with the next breath that he would put a stop to the disgrace; he would give the minister something to remember for his abominable presumption; he would let his sister know that she must take care what she was about so long as she bore his name and dwelt under his roof. But it must be all the old women's fault. Trust old women for cottoning to ministers, leading the humbugs and donkeys to make fools of themselves and show what they were really sweet upon. Old women of all classes and the clergy were like cooks and policemen. Bruce was too young for that sort of thing. And she knew what she was about. She knew her price, as his friend Lord Alexander had found to his cost. She could look after herself in a general way. She was game enough.

Lord Sandy shook his wicked head, snarled a secret snarl, and stirred again the furious rage and disgust which had been beginning to subside.

Claud cried he would go straight to the manse and call the minister to account.

'Better leave him to the ladies—that is, after you have set them right. They will dismiss him properly, without any risk run. Remember what an elephant this lap-dog is;' words which only added fuel to the fire, for Claud was no physical coward; on the contrary, he was fool-hardy in such an encounter as that he proposed.

'At least I would bide a wee, and let sleeping dowgs lie, Mr. Kirkpatrick,' recommended the horse-dealer, who, for his part, was anxious to promote peace, while the malicious scoundrel Lord Sandy was egging on the fray. 'There can be no harm in biding a bit. Matters may be susceptible of explanation.'

'There can be no explanation,' said Claud loftily, in the height of his haughtiness and towering wrath.

He ordered out his dog-cart, and drove—not straight in one sense, but in the style of driving of Jehu, the son of Nimshi—without turning aside, to the manse of Birkenbarns, leaving Lord Sandy to sneer, and the horse-dealer to suffer a salutary dread that, on the one hand a profitable customer's neck might be broken before its time; on the other, that the whole three men might be taken up as accessories in a case of aggravated battery and assault.

Arrived without an overthrow, by one of those miracles which seem to wait on the helpless, at the manse gate, into which Claud dashed like a whirlwind, the first person he met was Mrs. Baillie. She told him frankly a merciful man was merciful to his beast, but he had certainly overdriven his nag. No, the minister was not 'in;' and she did not think he would be back till the darkening.

'I'll wait for him,' said Claud, leaping down from his seat, leaving his panting horse to its fate as if he had a hundred as good in his stables, brushing past Mrs. Baillie unceremoniously, and when Sairey appeared bidding her show him to the study.

There, amidst the records of the gathered wisdom of ages, by the minister's desk, on which lay his half-written sermon, in the place where Wat and Rachie had often held high and sweet communion, the well-born clown, fool, and madman sank into the first chair. He breathed hard with exhaustion, while he brooded over the wrong done to his family pride and to the dignity of Bruce's gently born maidenhood, which, according to his light, the lad had always been scrupulous in guarding. As he brooded, he hugged his primitive project of punishment, fingering his riding-whip, and lying, as it were, in wait for his prey.

Mrs. Baillie and her maid, the only persons who had seen Claud's entrance, could not guess his errand; though Sairey asserted afterwards that her heart—probably influenced by a recollection too *à propos* of her late loud-tongued gossip—had come into her mouth at the young laird's aspect. 'He gloomed like a puttin' stot—nae less, though he's sae little buiket, beside the minister. A silly Tam Thoomb o' an ill-deedy laddie.'

Mrs. Baillie was one of the most dauntless

of women. She would hardly have hesitated, in the national phrase, to call the king her brother, or, more correctly, the queen her sister; but when she had followed the self-invited guest, after a short interval, into the study, and asked him, with a kind enough intention, if he would not come into the dining-room and take a cup of tea, she was sufficiently influenced by his short answer, and a traditional respect for the reigning laird of Birkencraig—far more powerful than any entertained for a hypothetical king or queen, to leave him in peace while he was meditating war.

Thus it happened that Claud sat on for more than an hour—a period of time which told against his case in the end; not wide awake all the time, but not sleeping sufficiently to restore in any degree the balance of his mind; dozing and starting, and getting if possible always more dazed and desperately inclined to fight with the first person he came across, above all to fall upon the big dolt and conceited dog of a minister, pommel him, knock him down, expose him to open contempt and derision, as a fit retaliation upon his most inpudent abuse of Bruce's silly thoughtlessness.

The gloaming was well advanced when Wat Baillie came into his manse by the side door, which in that quiet country-place was left conveniently and confidingly unbarred till supper-time. He had not been seen by any member of the family, and went first to his study without having been told of the visitor awaiting him there.

On the opening of the study door, Claud Kirkpatrick started up for the fifth or sixth time from momentary unconsciousness, with all his perceptions clouded and confused. He had no clear sense of where he was or what he was going to do. He felt only a burning irritability at being disturbed, added to the dim but dogged determination to get his revenge for the injury done to him and her, and for the miserable hour—or was it half-a-dozen hours?—he had been forced to spend in that hateful humbug of a minister's den.

Claud's chair happened to be in the shadow of the door, and Wat had not so much as set eyes on the intruder, when with the unnatural force lent by passion allied to madness the lad leapt up, dashed his arm in the face approaching him, and with the silver-mounted end of his whip struck the minister a crashing blow on the right temple and felled him insensible on the floor of his study. 'Take that for your low insolence to Miss Bruce Kirkpatrick!' the assailant cried to ears which did not hear. Then Claud flung his whip after the blow it had inflicted, stumbled over the prostrate figure, and walked out of the open door, before the members of the household, running together at the strange sound of the heavy fall, had recovered from their consternation at the state in which they found the minister.

Claud had regained his senses enough to trace his trap to the cart-shed, reclaim it from Lowrie Wilson, the minister's man, and help to re-yoke his horse. The assailant had driven away before one of the frightened, distressed family in the manse had so much as associated him with the calamity.

Rachie was less overcome at a really formidable crisis than she had been by the sight of the cut across her brother's wrist—now nearly whole—that evening in the garden.

Mrs. Baillie, after an involuntary sharp cry, 'My bairn! my bairn!'—all the more piteous because it was wrung from such a woman—showed herself strong to act out her notions of what ought to be done for her son in his need.

Tammas was still sufficiently able-bodied, with the help of the three women, to lift Wat on to the sofa.

'He must have over-walked himself,' said Rachie, with her voice sunk to a low, agonised whisper, 'fented, and struck his head in falling. But to think of our Wat fentin'! Oh! I wish he would speak. His een are not clean closed, but I dinna believe he sees us, though he's breathing loud enough, and I can feel both his heart and his pulse.'

It would have saved a wonderful amount of tribulation if Wat had been able to speak as Rachie wished or even to look intelligently around him, though it was not likely he would have substituted any other explanation than that his people had arrived at as to the nature of his accident. The truth was between the blow and the fall Wat Baillie had suffered concussion of the brain, and, most disastrously for all concerned, did not know what was passing around him, and could not take any active steps in his own affairs for the next twenty-four hours.

'He must have let his stamach gang terrible out o' order,' remarked Mrs. Baillie, in a louder, almost an angry key, bethinking herself of the amount of calomel she had in the house. 'I wonder if he can swally, though he doesna seem to see or hear? He must be got to take pheesic instantly.'

'Try him wi' a soup o' brandy,' suggested Tammas, 'the time me or Lowrie's saddlin' ane o' the plough horses and ridin' for the doctor.'

In order to bring about this conclusion a light was fetched, and then somebody's eyes first fell on Claud Kirkpatrick's whip lying where it had been launched, close by the door.

'What's that?'

'Whaur cam' that frae?'

'Wat has nae whup?' was repeated in bewilderment, and then a light flashed across Mrs. Baillie's mind and filled her with horror and rage. 'Gude forgive him, it has been that young villain Birkencraig that I spak' to at the door, and syne in this very room. Wat has been struck and felled in his ain hoose and hiz within cry. They have been argufying or fechten, gin ony decent lad—let-a-be a minister—would fecht wi' a young reprobate and diel's buckie like thon. But we heard no sound, till Wat, being a man o' peace, without even a cane in his hand, had the worst o't— a black shame! Awa', Tammas Bilie, awa', and lodge information wi' the police or the fiscal in Sauchope, as well as summon the doctor, or we'll have our puir braw laddie the minister o' the parish slain before our very een, and no satisfaction got, because the slayer is a prodigal laird come o' a race o' drunkards, scoffers, and scoondrels.'

'Oh! whisht! whisht! mither,' besought Rachie, 'you dinna ken how it cam' about. Wat thinks fair of the Kirkpatricks—the leddies o' them—ony gate. What would gar the laird commit sic a trespass—a terrible crime? There, there, the puir dear eelids have flickered.'

But the flickering was only momentary. Wat did not open his half-closed eyelids more widely or rouse himself to take part in the discussion which concerned him so nearly. All that Rachie gained by her interposition was a bitter reproach from her mother in which her father joined, of heartlessness and unnaturalness in having a word to utter in defence of the murderer of that brother whose greatest friend she had professed to be. The couple were rudely awakened from their cool conceit by the injury which had been done to their son. Their parental still more than their class blood was up. What did it matter, although they had not seemed to be too proud of Wat and had treated his attainments lightly, when both he and they were at the parents' command? The father and mother would prove their rights and their wrongs the moment they saw a finger had been raised against the pillar of the house, the pillar of the whole parish.

Before Wat knew what he was about or could prevent the step, the doctor had pronounced him seriously though not necessarily fatally hurt, by a stunning blow on the temple, which was much more likely to have come from the butt-end of a riding-whip wielded by cruelly reckless hands, than to have been caused by contact in falling with the corner of a door. In addition a very grave charge had been brought, and to a considerable extent substantiated, against Claud Kirkpatrick of Birkencraig. For the offence of which he was accused was a peculiarly detestable one in the eyes of early Scotch lawyers. It was known by the ancient name 'hamesucken,' which implies that the offender has rendered the deed of violence against a peaceful community doubly heinous, by deliberately seeking his victim in his home, and there in the house which ought to have been the unfortunate man's castle, dealing him wicked injury. If a man's own house is not to be reckoned safe and sacred, the old judges argued solemnly, what city of refuge can he fall back upon, since church sanctuary has been out of count, as a superstitious weakness, from the days of the Reformation? Therefore the Daniels exacted the utmost penalty of the law, short of a forfeited life, from the dishonourable regardless wretch, capable of the violation of all right feeling in the unnatural crime of 'hamesucken.' Even though the victim should recover, the sentence on the criminal might be transportation beyond the seas for life.

The undesirable comedy between the minister and Bruce Kirkpatrick, which had been awakening, unsuspected by the people most concerned as usual, a chorus of mingled ridicule and reprobation in the parish, was suddenly swallowed up in the awful delight of an apprehended tragedy. It did not detract greatly from the breathless satisfaction of a catastrophe, that public opinion in an agricultural parish in the main rampantly conservative, began immediately in the teeth of justice—prosaic or poetic, to set dead against the minister. Had Claud Kirkpatrick's lawless attack been more successful and either killed outright, or left the minister for many weeks in sore sickness and suffering and deadly peril, the rascally barbarity of the deed would have come conspicuously to the front, and taken men's minds by storm. Wat's many virtues would have been remembered, exalted to the skies, he would have been canonised without waiting a hundred years, and Claud Kirkpatrick would have been regarded forthwith with horror and loathing, as one who had committed sacrilege in addition to murder. But the whole business was a miserable bungle and compromise as well as a glaring anachronism. Wat Baillie was not killed or nearly killed; he was hardly even in much danger after the first twenty-four hours. No trembling suspense had to be met, no continuous stream of pity was called forth on his account, and this made all the difference in the world in his cause.

Claud Kirkpatrick was a *mauvais sujet*, but he was one of the old Kirkpatricks of Birkencraig who, with their good and evil, had in their turn belonged to the parish, while the parish had partly belonged to them for many a generation. He was the head of his house, the credit of which he had been seeking, however unwisely, to preserve. Certainly the most honourable point about him, in his far from honourable career, was his zeal for the credit of his young sister. Plenty of worthy people could sympathise with him on that head, while nobody could defend levity in a minister of the kirk. Bruce Kirkpatrick was but a girl, without father or mother to look after her and keep her under proper control. Mr. Baillie, who was her senior as well as her minister, ought to have been the first man to remember and respect her disadvantages, the last to employ them to her prejudice. So argued the stern righteousness, *esprit de-corps*, and not unmanly chivalry of the most of the fathers of young daughters, of whatever degree, in the parish.

'Weel-a-wat, a preacher o' th' word, and a dispenser o' ordinances, micht have had a hantle mair in his head than toyin' and fulin' wi' a young vain quean aboon him in station. What cam o' his meditations and prayers and makin' o' powerfu' sermons, his catechisin' o' the young, his mindin' o' puir folks' souls that are more precious in the een o' the Almichty than the ease and pleasure o' the rich and great that they set sic store on? We had ay a druther o' Wat Beelyie sin' he tuk up wi' the doctorin' o' the vile body. He was ower brodent from the first, on carnal learnin' and the interests o' this world; see to him fleein' like a gled at a godless newspaper as gin it had been a godly word o' a godly man of auld. They had been telled aforehand what would be the end o' sic a divided heart and how pride would get a fa'. No' that the minister was pridefu' in the ordinar' sense, only a thocht puffed up wi' his college and his books and sic weapons o' the flesh.' Thus spoke the old wives—those oracles of orthodoxy and devotion in Scotland, since the days of Jenny Geddes downwards.

There existed another much less powerful but still distinct and influential element in the tide which was turning against Wat Baillie's popularity. He had accepted the presentation to Birkenbarns, and come to it a young single man, who, in spite of such domestic dragons as his mother and Rachie, was a likely match for a large proportion of the disengaged young women in the parish. The facts of his humble birth and rearing among them, and his more familiar acquaintance, in consequence, with all ranks, had made the prize more open to a variety of claimants. Yet it is a rare event for a minister—of all the magnates risen from the people—to pay such heed to the Apostle James's injunction as to have no respect of persons, and to return to the class from which he sprang in order to draw from it a helpmeet in his manse, unless, indeed, he has committed himself by an early engagement. Either the charm of social refinement acts with peculiar power on him, or a sense of inexpediency gets the better of him, and he lets himself be persuaded that his usefulness will be seriously impaired if he go against the partialities and prejudices of the upper ten of his parishioners by bringing a peasant Dorothea to labour with him in his spiritual vineyard. But as we profess to believe that all men are equal in the sight of God, and that His religion more than any other force levels every difference of rank and training, it seems a pity that a few brave, honest men should not try the experiment, and ascertain whether the scandal of low-born, rustic, poor wives, to whom the husbands have stooped, would be really worse than the reproach of high-born, polished, rich wives, to whom the evangelists have aspired, making worldly stock and gain as it seems of their calling and graces and of women's well-known appreciation of such conditions and qualities. The result probably would be that some members of the higher classes would walk no more with their teachers, and some members of all ranks, estranged now, would turn and hear such disinterested authorities gladly. Where there are many candidates there must be many disappointed, and the tacit class rivalry here, together with the circumstance that Bruce Kirkpatrick had not been a recognised or fit candidate, and was not a general favourite, lent a bitterness to disappointment in the present instance. It was wrong-headed as well as mean in the minister to go hankering after Miss Bruce Kirkpatrick, a young lady who had not even taken a class in his Sabbath School, though she had been forward enough in displaying her ability in the new unwomanly capacity of serving as a doctor when occasion required. The verdict pronounced by the softest-hearted and humblest aspirant to the love of a large, reverent soul, and the privilege of being mistress of the manse of Birkenbarns, was that the minister was well served and richly deserved all that Claud Kirkpatrick had given him. 'No doubt, poor simple, learned fellow, he had been in the beginning misled and put upon '—with a little relenting to him, quickly atoned for by increased severity to her. 'Miss Bruce Kirkpatrick might be pleased with the mischief she had done. She was a high-spirited young lady, but this might satisfy even her ambition, that she had brought one man to the brink of the grave, and she had brought another—her own only brother—within the clutches of the law. She might, if she durst, go over to Birkenbarns, help to nurse her clerical admirer back to health, and demean herself to marry him, for nobody else would care to have a gift of him now.'

CHAPTER XI.

THE MINISTER 'WAITED UPON.'

NEVERTHELESS there did not fail faithful followers who clave to Muckle Wat, through good report and evil report, though it must be confessed they were the select few. The affair was sufficiently bad, but it might have been still worse, even without a charge of culpable homicide established against Claud Kirkpatrick by the death of the minister.

Miss Kirkpatrick and Miss Lily might easily have been overwhelmed by the dreadful blow —a double and triple blow to them. For it involved their family pride along with their family affection, especially their doting fondness for their old nursling, and it cut in a positively hopeless manner at the loyal allegiance of two good church-women who had taken the greatest interest in their kirk and their minister.

But the sisters, who, after all, had not been reared in the lap of indulgence, but had gone through a certain amount of hard experience under the old laird, rose to the occasion, and behaved with far more common sense than could reasonably have been expected from them, thus holding the misfortune in check, and lightening its disgrace.

Luckily Bruce had happened to be away from home for a few days, paying a visit to some cousins, when the outrage was committed. Her sisters, with the concurrence of their relations, absolutely interdicted her return, and decreed that she should remain where she was, till everything was settled and the whole unhappy business was blown over. They were not hard on what they knew of her folly, which, indeed, did not seem to them either very unusual or unpardonable. They could not be hard to anybody save 'a lady-doctoress.' But their instinct told them Bruce was better out of the way of the storm.

In other circumstances Bruce might have resisted the banishment indignantly; as it was, she was too confounded, affronted, and wretched to resist.

It had been found impossible to keep Claud from being taken before a magistrate; and while the minister of Birkenbarns was still lying in his manse stricken and incapable, from the effects of the treatment he had received, it was equally impossible for the most lenient justice to avoid committing the young man to stand a trial. He ought to have known better, and he had taken the law into his own hands on a piece of provocation, which, however it might strike sensitive, refined minds, was still a trifle in the eyes of the law. However, a point could be stretched in admitting the laird to bail, and plenty of bail was at his service.

The elder Misses Kirkpatrick would fain have had Claud back to be cried over, humoured, and bowed down to more than ever, but their nearest and wisest brother-in-law insisted, as the sisters had done in the case of Bruce, that Claud should be removed from the scene, and kept as far as possible out of the way, till he was wanted.

Claud had no objection, for though he was not sorry for his behaviour, which still appeared to him the most justifiable in the world, he was a little sick of the row which had been made and the mess which he had got into, when all the beggars, whether favourable or adverse, pulled such long faces, and the old girls threatened to become waterspouts. As for Bruce, of course he had acted like any other gentleman and done what was simply necessary, she must at all hazards be kept from running wild, getting herself talked about, and making a fool of herself, but he would rather not encounter his younger sister just at present. It would be awkward to meet other people who knew both him and that fellow of a minister, and might be trusted to discuss the story constantly out of his hearing. Lastly, his brother-in law lived in a good coursing county, and Claud desired to see coursing out of his own beat.

Mary and Lily Kirkpatrick had always deferred to male authority and opinion and to the inclinations of their darling. Thus the neighbourhood had a good riddance of both Bruce and Claud in the interval between the offence and the trial. A great deal of mischievous gossip was summarily stopped in the absence of the chief performers in the play, while the excitement was prevented from rising to anything like its highest pitch.

But though the worst had been avoided, very much that was bad and hard to bear remained, and Miss Kirkpatrick and Miss Lily could not so much as send for their minister and confer with him, profiting by his ghostly counsels. So far from that, the ladies could not even go to their parish church, and sit in the old family pew on Sundays, seeking strength and consolation at the proper place at the proper time, for this most unlooked-for, unexampled trial which had befallen them. From the melancholy night when they were told of poor dear Claud's rashness, the sisters knew that they could never enter again the church of their fathers, so long as the parish minister continued to be Wat Baillie. This in itself was a serious deprivation and grief to these simple conservative women. If they bore a heavy grudge against anybody concerned, it was against Wat Baillie, in spite of his punishment. But it was not so much for his misdemeanour, admitting that it was very blameworthy in a man of his birth and position, as for the ill-judged circumstances in which it had occurred that had led to its publicity—to its reaching Claud's ears—to all the trouble which had followed. With certain lingering recollections of their youth to influence them, it was on the last ground of complaint the two ladies dwelt chiefly.. For Tammas Baillie's son, the parish minister, to take it upon him to give Miss Bruce Kirkpatrick a kiss, was bad enough, no doubt; but if he was going to forget himself, what, in the name of decency and order, could tempt him to be guilty of the trespass in the manse garden, within sight of the windows? Could he not have waited till the two were in the house, in a room by themselves, or till he was escorting her home some night in the gloaming, and then, though it would still have been a most impertinent liberty in Wat Baillie, yet nobody save the couple need have been any wiser? It might have been a lesson to Bruce never to forget she was a Kirkpatrick, and however homely and charitable she chose to be, to keep herself, where familiar associates were in question, among her equals. If it had been a gentleman now, who had misbehaved as the minister had done, he would have taken care to misbehave in season, and not to expose a young lady to remark. Wat Baillie had conducted himself like the ploughmen from whom he had come.

It would have been vain to argue with the poor ladies that if deliberate precautions had been employed, they would have inferred that the offence was coolly premeditated, and so its turpitude would have been immensely aggravated.

Wat Baillie did not have it in his power to use any argument. He could have humbled himself and written any number of letters: of apology to the Misses Kirkpatrick if such a proceeding would have done any good, but he was sensible it would only add to the grievance. Unlike Claud Kirkpatrick, Wat Baillie was very sorry for his share in the wrong. What could he do to make up for it? he asked himself over and over again while he was still shaken and ill, with his head aching and giddy from the measure of chastisement Claud had inflicted on him.

Wat was not without natural resentment and indignation at the unmanly advantage which had been taken of him, the brutal attack made without warning on an unprepared, defenceless man on the threshold of his study. It was an attack which only the lack of stalwartness in Claud's arm, under Providence, or the good angels of both men, had saved from being murderous. He, the big, strong man, smarted under the mortification of having been felled to the ground by such a one as Claud Kirkpatrick. Still, Wat was too true and good to yield to his wounded pride and cherish a vindictive longing for revenge upon the ill-conditioned lad, who under a mistaken sense of family responsibility, had been the minister's assailant.

Rack his brains as he might, Wat was always brought up short by the miserable conviction that he could do nothing but bear the penalty of his absurdity and scandalous thoughtlessness. The matter had passed out of his hands from the moment the charge had been brought against Claud while Wat lay insensible. It was not he but the Crown that prosecuted. He was simply called upon, nay, compelled, to give his evidence as to what he knew of the facts of the case in which he figured so inappropriately. And even if the affair could still be hushed up, after what had come and gone, what would become of Bruce's part in it? Might not what had been the merest inconsiderateness bred of her innocent girlishness, and leading to nothing worse than a piece of rough, unmannerly retaliation, be so twisted and tortured under the coarse, malignant handling of slander as to signify something widely different? He recoiled in anguish and horror from her best inheritance of a spotless reputation being put in peril by his means. Even without the risk of this terrible punishment for a small offence, in which he was the guiltier person, was not the truth always and in all circumstances best? Wat had such a reverence for the truth, that he could not even comprehend loyalty either to God or woman without it. He was not tempted to lie in order to shield Bruce Kirkpatrick; on the contrary, to brace himself to tell the foolish truth was the greatest service he could render her. But even if a lie could have saved her from suffering, it would have been to him a double falsehood, a witless blunder. Truth was the one element of human history which proved sure and lasting. The very devil was shamed by the truth, according to the popular adage. Tell the truth, undo whatever was done amiss, and be at peace with God, one's self, and the world for ever after. There was neither confidence, nor rest, nor stability in any other course. The truth was like the white beams of light in which every incident could be seen in its genuine character and just proportions. It might be an awkward, a painful, in some cases an awful ordeal to speak the truth, but speaking it was the one hope and safeguard of individuals and of the race. Wat had not the least doubt of the vital importance of the truth on all subjects, secular and sacred. What perplexed, hurt, and mortified him was the very different standard which even respectable people held of the truth: how in sport or in earnest they could, in spite of their conventional codes of honour, with the greatest ease, speak and act a lie equivocal whenever their affections, interests, or even their amusements became implicated.

Without even waiting to see the falling off of his parishioners from him, Wat felt often very downhearted under the cloud. He was driven to speak hard things against himself— almost to believe that he had sinned in a moment of levity against his calling, so as to render it advisable for him to lay down his commission, or at least resign the parish of Birkenbarns, dear to him from the first as the place of his birth and the scene of his boyhood. It had been growing dearer and dearer to him every day as the field of his labours; but he was sometimes fain to think he ought to turn his back upon it in earnest, as Bruce had threatened in jest she would make him do. Perhaps it would be better for him to go at once and offer himself as a foreign missionary. In distant lands it was to be hoped no hint of the escapade which had cost him dear would ever reach the ears of his yellow, copper-coloured, or black flock. And even if it did so, among the enormities of heathens and of exiled Christians who have forgotten their Christianity in all save the name, his momentary unclerical performance would sound venial indeed.

But Wat was a healthy natured man, gifted with grace. He could not long exaggerate extravagantly. An instant's folly, however disastrous the effects, ought not to be regarded as a deadly sin. To throw up his license would be morbid, even egotistical weakness, unworthy of the Master whom he served, and the calling to which he belonged. To abandon his parish, in place of living down all the mistakes and errors he was sure to commit, and the many falls he was certain to suffer in the course of his career—unless it were destined to be of the briefest, would be sheer cowardice, however it might shield itself under the high-sounding titles of magnanimity and disinterestedness. If he was not fit to address well-informed people, he was still less fit to instruct untaught heathen. The more difficult the task, the higher ought to be the qualification. He who was willing to become an exile, perhaps a martyr, for Christianity, should be without the shadow of reproach or the suspicion of interested motives. He who joined the missionary ranks in order to skulk from his creditors, cut the knot of a dilemma, or escape from a scandal, was unworthy the name of missionary, and no good could come of his work. To retreat from the full penalty, and leave Bruce Kirkpatrick to bear it alone, would be grossly unfair to her.

Little or nothing has been said as yet of the state of Wat Baillie's feelings towards Bruce, which might have contributed to bring about the present predicament, and would without fail influence him in his efforts to set it right. The truth is, in spite of the vast number of novels which would have made such sentiments the prominent controlling forces of the history, Wat's feelings with regard to Bruce were by no means the active factors in the business which they might have been expected to be. His feelings were about as vague and indefinable as hers. There was certainly a mutual attraction between the two—the attraction of reverses and the attraction of similitudes also. On his side there was a tender indulgence—not always in accordance with reason—for the little Miss Bruce to whom he had looked up with the wonder and admiration of a big, uncouth, reverential boy. This tenderness inflicted on him the keenest pang for the trouble he had brought upon her.

On her side, there was a struggling, earnest respect for the man and the minister, contending with a habitual slighting estimation of Muckle Wat Baillie with his obtrusive ears.

The state of his mind was further complicated by his fervent repentance for having injured her.

The state of hers implied the still more dubious condition of an undisciplined yet candid and generous nature, which while angry and aggrieved cannot deny its own unwarrantable sin of provocation, so as to take up an attitude of implacability.

If there had been an opportunity of meeting where the couple were concerned, it would have furnished embarrassment to the verge of distress to both. He would have been ready to abase himself, solicitous to express his deep unfeigned regret, while at the same time his old unconsciousness and calm politeness would have given place to an agitation that threatened to render him dumb, and a timidity which shrank from annoying her farther.

She would have taken high ground, looking stones or daggers, all the while keeping up a pretence of callous imperturbability or even insulting gaiety, for the benefit of the public in general.

But if either of these demonstrations meant love, it was only the shy, dim dawn of love rudely dispelled and forced into unnatural development.

Wat Baillie had not possessed the excuse, such as it was, of ungovernable passion for the freedom he had indulged in. For that matter, it might strike most people who are not either shallow or vulgar, that if a man like Wat had been devotedly in love with Bruce Kirkpatrick, the very last thing he could have done would have been exactly what he did do. His offence was a breach of manners, not an outburst of emotion.

In his own house Wat, from the moment he became aware of his unhappy plight, found a divided family. His mother, and his father led by his mother, when they had discovered the cause of the laird's attack, and were relieved from the dread of a fatal end to it, resented it on their son as if he had been foolish on purpose to affront them, no less than to bring a slur on his coat. Mrs. Baillie sniffed, groaned, and improved the occasion, and Tammas echoed her groans, till Wat, good son though he had always been, was well-nigh goaded into becoming a prodigal so far as forsaking his father and mother went. Only Rachie stood by him, modest, sedate Rachie, who had never altogether liked Miss Bruce Kirkpatrick, and had foreboded some catastrophe from their familiar acquaintance.

Rachie even put force on herself to make light of the deed. 'To give a wild lassie a bit kiss to stop her mouth for a minute, what ferlie was that to make sic an outcry about? The gentry were not so strait-laced on their own account. It would be well for them if no heavier or more shameful sin could be laid to their charge. No doubt Wat was a minister, but he was also a man—a young man who would grow wiser and never lose his head or be carried away by fun and nonsense again. And what was Miss Bruce Kirkpatrick that the touch, like the brush of a butterfly's wing, of Wat's pure lips was to work her such harm? She might contract baser soil before she was out of this world.'

There was much talk as well as smothered laughter (tell it not in Gath!) among the Rev. Wat's reverend brethren at his extraordinary scrape, a lively variation on disputes with heritors and whispers of heresy, the usual stumbling-blocks of ministers in Scotland. But even although there had been a malicious rival willing to do a bad turn to a man with his back temporarily at the wall, the case was clearly not one for the Presbytery.

But the divided, distracted state of the parish with the alarming prospect of one of the principal parishioners being subjected to a public trial in a criminal court, admittedly by the fault of the minister, was as clearly a question for the Kirk Session, with which the Rev. Wat had hitherto worked so harmoniously. It was an indication of this that the members, instead of calling on their head to summon a formal meeting in the crisis, with the customary readiness in dealing with a scandal, showed their reluctance to incriminate their minister and even their delicacy in approaching the subject, by preferring to appoint a deputation to call upon him and confer with him in the manse privately.

Wat was grateful for their forbearance and consideration. He felt anxious in the middle of a sore sense of pain and humiliation, which he told himself sternly was no more than his desert, to give his office-bearers all the satisfaction in his power, and to submit as far as he could honestly to their decision.

He received the Elders—consisting of the

laird, one of the farmers, and the riddle-maker—in his study, formerly the scene of so much peace and happiness, with gravity befitting the occasion, but also with a cordial welcome signifying his comprehension of their friendly meaning.

Whatever the Elders' shortcomings might be, or however they might act, they were worthy, well-intentioned men, all of them, as Wat knew to his comfort, in anticipation of this trying interview. He felt that the traditionary prayer which he, with so many Scotch ministers, had been in the habit of 'putting up' every Sunday, that these men 'who bore the vessels of the sanctuary' might be pure, had been largely answered. He was thankful that at the most solemn moment in the services of his church, when he addressed his immediate followers in the time-honoured words 'the Elders will now bring in the elements,' no painful sense of incongruity could be aroused unless among the thoroughly contumacious, the 'ill-doers' who are also the 'ill-dreaders.' There was no reasonable call for a heavy stumbling-block to be found in the spectacle which presented itself when these mature, mostly grey-headed men of all ranks, in their sober yet full dress suits—uniform so far as black coats and white ties went—came in with measured step and reverent mien like men impressed by the dignity of their duties, and yet with the sedate composure of servants who had voluntarily accepted their responsibility, bearing flagons, cups, and plates. These were sometimes of precious metal and old fine workmanship, handed down in the parish for centuries, sometimes of modern, homely enough material, but always containing the symbols of bread and wine, the substitute for the Host before which, as it is borne by a simple village priest on a country road, or by a bishop beneath a canopy in the principal street of a great capital, every knee is bent and every face veiled in Roman Catholic Christendom. These ordinary laymen—some of them as unlettered as any Scotchman can be—represented the twelve apostles in carrying round the bread and wine to the different 'tables,' and offering them in succession to each intending communicant. The gallant hero Sir Ralph Abercromby solemnly declared that he was prouder of being elected an Elder of his parish kirk than of any of the laurels with which war had crowned him. And it had been a lawful source of pride to Wat Baillie that no single-minded sharer in the ordinance could object to the clean hands which transmitted its sign.

Though the riddle-maker, who was a bony, cadaverous man, was, with his gift of speech, generally the first to begin a discussion, he sat with a hand on each knee and a face inclined downwards, leaving the laird to open the ball to-day; while the polemical farmer, a short, vigorously compact person, turned his shoulder on the other three, and stared fixedly out of the window nearest to him.

The laird, with his long back, high nose, and sensitive mouth, thus thrust into the front, did his best to respond to the sudden trust reposed in him, and not to collapse under the awkwardness of the situation, and what might be the false dictates of good breeding in a gentleman's difficulty in dealing with such a matter, and interfering in what was certainly the private affair of another man.

There were a few preliminary observations, beginning with the inevitable irrelevant remarks on the weather, and proceeding to more pertinent inquiries after Wat's health. These did not imply that his Elders had not asked for their minister before; on the contrary, they had been in frequent, though separate and unofficial anxious attendance at the manse during the worst of his illness. The preliminaries ended with a still more significant interrogation whether he would venture to preach on the next Sabbath; to which Wat answered firmly in the affirmative.

Then the riddle-maker coughed faintly and looked up and across at the laird, while the farmer stirred on his seat.

'Mr. Baillie,' began the laird, in a voice which actually shook, for he had a nervous constitution, 'I presume you guess the object— I may say the painful object—of our visit?'

Wat bowed with a heightened colour, but hastened to add, 'And you will allow me to say, gentlemen, that I am very glad to see you. I thank you for this mark of confidence in coming to me.' As he said it, with the old-fashioned stateliness which formed the warp to the woof of what was homely in his manner, sitting there big and still, it seemed impossible to bring against a scholar and divine the most frivolous of accusations.

But this was what Mr. Fowler, the laird of Murniepae, had to do, and there was no backing out of the task. Indeed, he never thought of it. He was a remarkably conscientious man, though not particularly clear-headed or long-sighted. 'There is no use in attempting to beat about the bush,' he went on, labouring to keep calm and matter-of-fact while struggling with excitement. 'We are all only too well aware that a very disagreeable, I may call it grievous, quarrel has arisen in the parish with which you, sir, are unhappily mixed up; in fact, I fear a false step of yours has been most unfortunately the origin of the whole matter.'

'I beg your pardon, Mr. Fowler,' said the farmer, facing round abruptly, and speaking as if the laird were beating about the bush;

'before we go any farther I should just like to ask the minister the plain truth of the story.'

Wat bent his head again, as if he had said 'You are entitled to it, and you shall have it.' It was by his own idiotic deed he had subjected himself to being sat upon and cross-examined by his Elders. The process was exquisitely disconcerting and vexatious to all concerned; but the inquisitors were not intentionally rendering it insufferable. He was bound to submit to the indignity as many would feel it.

The laird thus called to order, and summoned from the roundabout to the straightforward mode of interrogation, hurried on with a startling jerk to the core of the question: 'Is it true, sir, that you kissed Miss Bruce Kirkpatrick?'

'Yes, I did, I am sorry to say,' answered Wat with a quietness which was no test of his contrition, but rather of the force put upon himself in the admission, while he knit his brows and his lips whitened perceptibly.

'Confessed like a man,' the farmer was saying to himself.

'Puir frail mortals!' the riddle-maker was moralising.

But the laird, though he had been compelled to believe the report from the first, since the story could not have attained the dimensions it had taken without some foundation, rather resented, whether from caste prejudice or from some more occult cause, Wat's instant unqualified admission of his offence. He spoke again with sharpness. 'May I ask if you are engaged to be married to the young lady?'

'No, I am not,' replied Wat instantly.

'Or is there any probability of your becoming engaged?'

'Not that I know of,' answered Wat a little oddly, as if he were staggered by being so pushed, and as if he asked, in turn, would the latter contingency afford any apology for the trespass?

The laird had been undergoing a sliding scale of provocation. Every word Wat spoke tended, in spite of him, to irritate Mr. Fowler still farther, till he was fairly incensed, for the good man had a fiery temper. 'Mr. Baillie, you are my clergyman, and you have been my friend; but let me, an old man, tell you, a young man, what you do not seem to see for yourself. Your conduct was most indefensible. You have created a scandal in the parish, and brought a stigma on the Church. You have driven a young gentleman to seek a rash remedy for what he considered, justly, an insult to his sister and a wrong to his family; which may end in farther and still deadlier wrong. What he did on a momentary impulse of outraged affection and natural—even praiseworthy—resentment, may bring down on him a cruelly heavy punishment.'

'Canny, laird, canny!' besought the riddle-maker.

'Surely we are not here to defend Mr. Claud Kirkpatrick's unlawful violence,' exclaimed the farmer with some heat. He was one of the sprinkling of democrats in the parish, and had a standing pique at lairds, not excepting his own laird. Besides, he was always ready to fight the very stones of the wall for what he regarded as the right side in a dispute. Since he approved on the whole of Wat's demeanour, he naturally turned upon his brother-Elder.

'Mr. Fowler,' Wat interposed hastily, 'you are perfectly right; and nobody can be more willing than I to admit that my behaviour was ungentlemanlike.'

'Houts!' muttered the riddle-maker. 'We have nought to do with what is ungentlemanlike; it is what is Christianlike we ha'e come aboot.'

The grand old name of gentleman had

clearly been misapplied in Andrew Sandiland's hearing.

'It was quite indefensible,' Wat was going on to grant in sad fullness of confidence. 'I do not know what induced me to be so foolish, but my rearing was not refined. The lassie teased me, and I gave her a kiss, before she or I knew what she was about, to silence her,' he said, half speaking to himself, with a partial return to the vernacular.

'Eh! man; what for did ye no resist the Enemy, and he would ha'e floon frae ye?' put in the riddle-maker in wistful reproach.

But Wat took no notice as he hurried to get done with his confession. 'That is the short and long of the story. It was very thoughtless and wrong. I forgot my cloth, I forgot her position, the example I was bound to show, the tongues that might wag. No one can be more distressed than I am. I would give half of my goods to undo a moment's folly. I would cut off my right hand rather than that Claud Kirkpatrick should come to harm by my means.'

'Well and stoutly spoken, Minister!' exclaimed the farmer loudly and defiantly, as if he would have liked to spring up and 'clap' Wat on the back. Indeed, Wat's champion told the farmer's family afterwards it would have melted the heart of a stone to hear a grand man like the minister own to a lad's fault with a child's simplicity and pain. 'The best of us is liable to err, and nobody, however bigotted '—he pronounced the word with the accent on the second syllable, and meant prejudiced, not fanatical, with an intended rebuke to the laird—' can refuse to own that you have been frank in your explanation, and made all the amends in your power.'

The laird, too, was touched and practically disarmed by the not unmanly meekness and singleness of heart with which Wat had received his censor's strictures and offered his explanation. Mr. Fowler was a generous man in his recurring excitability. 'It is a most unfortunate business,' he said, wiping his forehead, and speaking still with perturbation though much more placably. 'But I hope and trust the ferment and bad feeling will blow over, and the threatened schism come to nothing after all. I am not here to make matters worse. If I have said anything, Mr. Baillie, which we could wish unsaid, you must attribute it to the esteem in which I have always held my minister, and the gratification I derived from what looked the very flourishing condition of Christianity in the parish, so that I have beheld with the greater grief the blight that has overtaken our prosperity. But I am bound to agree with my fellow-Elder '—he spoke a little stiffly here—'that you, sir, have been perfectly frank with us. And when a man, be he minister or layman, gentle or simple, allows that he has been in the wrong, is sorry for it, and will avoid such temptations in future, when that is all the reparation possible in the circumstances, I do not see that anything more can be required of him. I suggest that, so far as the Kirk Session has to do with the case, no farther notice should be taken of it, though it must attain the miserable notoriety of a secular law court.'

'And I propose as an amendment,' declared the farmer, forgetting that he was not at a regularly constituted meeting, 'that we enter in our minutes in fit and proper language that we find the clash arose from a trifle—not worth a bawbee or half a thought in a reasonable being's mind. We hold that we have no good ground for disapproving—far less censuring—the minister's conduct. On the contrary, we maintain that a most monstrous, dastardly outrage ——'

'No, no, Mr. Dunlop; you must not say or

write that,' cried Wat, won to a smile, the first he had smiled that day, by the zeal of his adherent. 'If I have your forgiveness for what is past and your sympathy in the ordeal which is yet to come, it is more than enough, far more than I have any title to expect.'

The laird was not grudging when he had begun to concede the difference. 'You shall have that, sir. I think I may promise your Elders will stand by you. It is some comfort to know we can still work together, and in time look forward to bygones being bygones.'

'There's no mistak that the whole stramash is a dispensation of Providence to mind us we're but sinfu' dust and ashes, and keep us from erecting idols, and being uplifted because of the number of our members and the size of our classes. If you hae nae objection, sirs, I wad have somebody put up a bit of prayer before we part, beseechin' the Almighty to order and improve the dispensation for His glory and our gude, and to bring and keep us a' in the richt gait henceforth.'

'With all my heart, Mr. Sandilands,' said Wat. He always called his Elder 'Mr. Sandilands' when the latter was acting in any way officially, though the minister was in the habit of dropping into 'Andrew' when he bought the riddle-maker's riddles, 'and do you, who have had the grace to think of it, put up the prayer.'

Before the Nathaniel had ended his quaint, earnest petition, and the petitioners had risen from their knees, peace and goodwill were restored among them. Wat Baillie's session-house was not destined to become a stronghold of his enemies. At the same time Wat was inclined to judge, just as some of us think the bitterness of death is past for us after we have been forced to meet the last enemy in the persons of those dearer than our own souls, that after having faced the deputation of his

Elders on this delicate question, he could face any court in the kingdom—and he at least was right.

The court implied a multitude, but it was for the most part a strange multitude, not the familiar faces which had been wont, even where the laird and the polemical farmer were concerned, to defer and look up to the minister. The crowd which assembled to hear the interesting details of a laird's having 'thrashed' his parish minister to the point of insensibility, with risk to life, because the minister had kissed the laird's sister, did not come under the head of the crowd, in which many women of all ranks bear a part, that has become a prominent ominous feature in recent trials for murder. There it would seem that the spectacle of a human creature at bay in the hardest, last extremity short of the hangman's hands, has taken the place of a bull-fight or a gladiatorial show, as a welcome sensation to jaded, brutalised imaginations. This was a crowd that collected from all sides, not for a tragedy, but for a comedy, out of sheer love of diversion, because of the comicality, irrespective of the torture which might lie under the fun. It was a crowd that came to jeer and giggle, and for the most part it did jeer and giggle to its heart's content, undeterred even by the judge's formal reprimand, and the usher's mechanical 'Silence!' Had not the judge and usher been themselves grinning the moment before? For there are allusions which are sure to provoke a laugh in public though they can be heard in private without eliciting the ghost of a smile. The minister of Birkenbarns had to answer some of the awkward questions he had answered to his Elders, and the slight, sickly lad at the bar was proved to have felled the big man in the witness-box. It was all superlatively absurd, no doubt, and only exceptional persons in the audience not closely connected with the case, who might have joined in the general merriment for a moment, looked beyond the laughter and reached regions above and beneath it. These spectators contemplated the style of Wat's presence, and the pallor and flush which rose in succession to his brow, and grew grave. Then they looked at the half-blustering, half-sulky, puny youngster opposed to Wat Baillie with his fine physique. Claud Kirkpatrick's wandering, blood-shot eyes were never caught and fixed in an honest answer to an inquiring glance. His entire aspect bore traces of desperate dissipation and degradation. The humane, high-minded gazers grew graver still as they looked.

By the greatest effort and influence Bruce had not been called on to appear in the witness-box. In the same manner the whole strength of Claud's counsel had been employed so that the very name and nature of the ancient crime of 'Hamesucken' should be left out of the case, and the charge should be confined to assault with hostile intent.

Even after the success of the manœuvre and all the gloss which could be put on the affair, by dwelling pathetically upon the jealousy of an attached brother with regard to the slightest injury done to a young orphan sister, of whom he was the natural guardian and defender, the best lawyer in practice could not have prevented a jury's finding the charge proven and the prisoner guilty. And not the most lenient judge with the most aristocratic bias could have pronounced a more merciful sentence than six months' imprisonment, if law were not to dwindle into a mockery.

The prisoner was quickly withdrawn from the court, to drown his petulant, ungrateful, idiotically arrogant protest that he had been done and sold by the whole pack—advocates, jury, and judge. The country was coming to a pretty pass when a gentleman could not call a clerical cub like Baillie to account for a piece of cursed insolence to a lady and a Kirkpatrick, without being disgracefully served.

The Reverend Wat retired hanging his head. He would need all the support of his Elders, all the stay of a conscience void of any other offence save that of a moment's levity. For though he might convict himself of folly, he could not accuse himself of falsehood, meanness, time-serving, or intentional wrong to any human being.

CHAPTER XII.

'TIRLING AT THE PIN.'

'THEY might as well have killed Claud at once!' the elder Miss Kirkpatrick cried out in despair. Talk of manslaughter! It would be Claud who would be slain in cold blood because he had loved his sister and stood up for her like a man against a shameful advantage taken of her thoughtlessness, with all the ill-natured gossip which was sure to spread abroad. Was Claud a fit person for a prison? It made their blood run cold and broke their hearts to think of it. And when had a Kirkpatrick been named in the same breath with a gaol since Jacobite times, when the laird of that generation had lain with his peers in the Tower under a charge of high treason?

But the mourners were a little soothed when they learned that the sentence might be regarded as nominal in many respects. Claud would not be put in the prison dress, or subjected to hard labour or prison fare; therefore the imprisonment need not be held an indelible stain. Doubtless the governor would be brought to wink at the ladies driving over to the county town almost every day of the week, carrying with them all the dainties the sisters could think of or Claud could fancy, for their pet. The prison was in a most healthy situation; it was dreadful to have to think of that in relation to Claud, still the Misses Kirkpatrick need not refuse to be thankful that the place had the highest character for salubrity. As to the term of the sentence, it was sure to be shortened on account of the delicacy of the prisoner's constitution and the extent to which he was certain to suffer from confinement.

It all came about as hopeful friends and satellites had ventured to predict. Claud Kirkpatrick enjoyed exceptional fame and importance, without many drawbacks, in the county gaol. If he was not exactly fêted, he was visited and condoled with, both by equals and inferiors, in the most attentive manner. Prison rules were considerably relaxed on his account. Even respectable elderly ladies—though Claud would have little to say to them—who were in the habit of visiting on religious and philanthropic errands, a very different style of prisoner, were smitten by the sorry enough grains of chivalry and romance, together with the glamour of superior rank in the offence and the offender. They had their tender hearts so softened towards the young fellow who had been a wild madman for his fatherless young sister's sake, that they would have done anything for his comfort and for the beguiling of the irksomeness of his stay in their sphere. He lent a wonderful interest to what they had elected to be their life-work, therefore they were bound to repay him. They did not presume to offer him tracts, but the ladies were proud to send, with a delicious pretence of secrecy, a choice of their most comfortable easy-chairs for his use, and to smuggle into the governor's care the most toothsome preserves in their cupboards for Claud's delectation. In addition, the gentle owners proposed to lend the interesting youth the liveliest tales in their libraries of street Arabs. It is needless to say Claud did not want the easy-chairs or preserves, and never looked into the annals of the Arabs.

The commutation of Claud's sentence took place at the end of the first three months, when he had grown thoroughly tired of the variety in his life which being locked up had afforded him. The doctor certified that his health, such as it was, had begun to give way, and an order of release was signed, to the jubilation of all save the prison authorities, to whom the period of Claud's incarceration had been an agreeable interlude.

There could not be two dispassionate opinions on the question, that by far the heavier share of the penalty for the offence fell on the minister. It was not that his health suffered permanently; it might have been better for him, in more lights than one, if it had. But long before the trial he was as well and powerful-looking as ever, which had enabled Claud's counsel—in spite of medical evidence, which, to be sure, does not go for much in courts of law—to point the finger of scorn at any assertion that his client had done more than knock down the minister of Birkenbarns in the gentlest, well-nigh facetious fashion of that ordinarily not too gentle and jocular performance. And there was nothing like general pity for any other injury worse than bodily harm which Wat Baillie might have suffered. Claud Kirkpatrick's imprisonment was a tangible evil, but any disappointment and misery endured by Wat were far beyond the range of common sympathies. The minister had failed in his high calling; he had proved a source of strife instead of a peacemaker. There was what the Laird of Murniepae had called a slur upon him, a drag upon all his future movements. Though he preached even more earnestly and carefully than ever, his once well-filled church became more and more deserted. The noble patron who had presented Wat with the living was at home for a season; but, disgusted with the unheard-of difficulty into which his man had got, he did not choose to bestow his countenance on the culprit, but continued the languid, fitful attendance at the Episcopal Church he was wont to give when away from Birkenbarns. Thus the parish and the kirk of Scotland lost one of the few noblemen that were left to them. The Kirkpatricks were the next in the order of lairds, and of course their pew remained vacant; others of the upper class considered themselves bound to resent the sin against caste, though the Laird of Murniepae, with the other Elders, continued faithful to his allegiance. Several tenant-farmers on the Birkencraig estate—partly from an old feudal feeling, still more from policy—began to drop off from the parish kirk and wander off to other kirks, whose ministers did not decline to make them welcome. For, alas! more than one of Wat's brethren who had laughed at his trouble, when they saw to what it had led, caring a good deal for the opinion of men, took to showing him a cold shoulder, while they did not refuse to benefit by his loss. A portion of the misinformed labouring class—though not, of course, the paupers, who represent a permanent institution in a parish—departed with their employers.

It was at this time that a party of strangers, happening to be in Wat's kirk listening to one of his heartfelt, eloquent sermons, preached to the next thing to bare walls, expressed their surprise that the preacher was not better appreciated even by stolid, bucolic intellects, and received the astounding explanation in an ambiguous version of the style of the House that Jack built: This was the minister that had kissed the laird's sister, that had been thrashed by the laird, that had lain in gaol for the deed.

Wat was terribly disheartened. He had thought that he sat lightly by public favour; but when it was withdrawn from him, when his parishioners were shrinking and dwindling away before his eyes, and his friends were turning their backs upon him, he could have told a different tale.

It would seem as if his father and mother, in spite of their complacent philosophy, had been inordinately vain of their son's social standing and influence, so deeply did they resent his downfall, so constantly did they visit it on him in aspersions and reflections, which held him up in his own eyes as little better than a hypocrite and black sheep among ministers. 'Ay, my man, your tricks ha'e brocht ye to a fine pass,' his mother would tell him austerely. 'Better ye had sticket afore ye entered the poopet. How can ye ever haud up you're head there again, when you ha'e been blecket for idle daffin', like ony graceless lad. More by token ye ha'e caused a puir silly callant o' a laird to be thrown into jail for the best turn he ever played in seekin' to look after his ain gypsy o' a sister. Ye ha'e broken their friends' hearts. I'm wae to think a son o' mine—man-muckle, wi' his wisdom teeth cut, let-a-be a minister—could be sae licht in the head.'

'Mother,' cried Wat, appealing in desperation to old fellow-feeling and momentary weakness, 'did my father never steal a kiss from you in your courting days?'

Mrs. Baillie turned sternly upon her son. 'You're no blate lad to mint that to your mither. Tammas Bilie kenned better what becam him and me than to presume ower far, and he was not a preacher o' the gospel, no to say an ordained minister, who ocht to have been like a licht set on a can'lestick or a hill. Neither are you makin' up in earnest to Miss Bruce Kirkpatrick; od if the young laird thocht that, he would not stick at murderin' you, there's sic spunk in the waikly body o' him.'

'He had better try it again,' said Wat grimly; then he called himself to order. 'No, of course, there is no thought of that,' he said hastily, in a lower tone, and with a sigh, in answer to her implied question.

'It would be simple Jockys and Jennys who would come and listen ony mair to your lectures and expositions, no to say your prayers, after sic wark,' his mother assured him coolly. 'I'm thinkin' ye had better gied up and try a scule, if your character will stand that muckle exem, and if your ill-name dinna gang afore you and hang you.'

'Weel, Wat, I thocht to ha'e done my pairt to your glebe,' groaned his father; 'but gin the nowt ha'e run through your repitation as a minister, you may e'en tak your mither's advice. The bonnie fields maun gang with the kirk and manse afore we ha'e gotten a bushel for a' the gude dung I ha'e putten into the lan'.'

Rachie never flinched from her brother, but she, like himself, was unduly depressed by the misfortunes which undoubtedly he had brought upon himself. She was nearer being crushed along with him, than capable of cheering him by an elastic spirit, and a faith that would not falter.

When the news came that Claud Kirkpatrick was free and coming home, a new idea laid hold of his partisans, for a faction had come into being on his behalf. They would give him a welcome home to wipe off the little stain of his imprisonment, and show they thought he had been badly treated, while the demonstration would serve as an additional sign of their determined and lasting condemnation of the minister.

As the reception awarded to Claud was not to begin till the prison bounds were passed, there could be no official interference with the pretty plan. Some of the wiser of Claud's family friends did look coldly on the suggestion which was, in fact, a defiance of the sentence of the law. They made an attempt to extinguish the proposal in its first sparks, but this prudent conduct only fanned the enthusiasm of the more foolish into a brighter flame. Unfortunately, the idea chimed in only too well with the weakness of the elder Misses Kirkpatrick. Mary and Lily had entirely lost sight of the fact that Claud had been condemned and sentenced justly for a crime against law and society. They did not require to be persuaded that their neighbours fully agreed with them in regarding their boy as an innocent victim, the next thing to a hero, and a very fair substitute for that rare and often uncomfortable production. They were full of inconsiderate joy as over Claud's triumph. There was something half piteous, half provoking in their delusion. All the concession that the more upright and sensible spirits on Claud's side could gain, was that there should be no public allusion to the minister, no hissing or groaning at him, no resort to the manse with the purpose of burning his effigy under his nose. Miss Kirkpatrick and Miss Lily saw the propriety of the reservation, on their sister's account if for nothing else, that her share in the story might, if possible, slip into the background of people's minds. But, indeed, they were not vindictive women, and were quite sincere in solemnly assuring whoever cared to listen that they wished no harm to Wat Baillie. It could not be called harm to desire that his eyes might be opened to the gross solecism he had committed, and that he might be sorry for all the worry and distress he had occasioned. But the past was happily over, when a public honour should atone to Claud for a public affront, so that the last might be clean wiped out. As good Christians, therefore, the Misses Kirkpatrick forgave Wat Baillie, though it was not to be thought they could ever speak to him again, or re-enter the church of Birkenbarns during the tenure of his ministry. It was inconvenient, and still felt, somehow, strange and wrong, to drive a mile and a half farther to Muirend Church on Sundays and to have Mr. Fraser instead of the ladies' parish minister to any 'dinner party' over which they had still a chance of presiding. But this state of matters could not be helped.

Thus the manse and its occupants were left to as much peace as they could be expected to feel, when they were thoroughly acquainted with the circumstances. Claud Kirkpatrick's friends and neighbours were to take advantage of the termination of his imprisonment, to meet and escort him home, as if he had been returning from the wars, or were bringing back a bride, which would be the next reason for rejoicing no doubt. And there was to be a great entertainment at Birkencraig afterwards.

The afternoon and evening dragged out slowly at Birkenbarns with a markedly uncomfortable sense of the family having been sent to

Coventry, and shut out of a natural connection with what was going on within a short distance of them. The very topic which was engrossing everyone, though he and she happened to be absent from the singular festival, was tacitly shunned in the Baillie household—only Mrs. Baillie diversified the dulness of the time by sundry reminiscences of parish doings, in which the minister had always played a prominent part ending by an assertion which nobody contradicted, 'Weel-a-weel, it's a fell change. I daresay there has na been, what may be called a public denner in the place, at which the minister has na said grace and returned thanks—no since my mither's day, when there was a drucken minister who had to be deposed before his first year was out.'

Wat's first year was out, but how many more years he was to spend there, or if he were to fulfil another in the grand service, in which he had hoped to end his days, it would have been hard to say. If his people melted away like snow before the first spring sunshine, he could not stay on to be a permanent stumbling-block among them.

At last the March evening closed in and drew to an end. The weather was dull and depressing. The cold had strengthened as the day lengthened. There was little promise even of a primrose, and the Craig still bore a patch of snow, sodden and splashed by ineffectual rain on its disconsolate head. The one comfort was that darkness soon hid the cheerless landscape. The Books were brought in, the herrings were eaten, Wat, with a sigh of relief, received his mother and father's last good night, and was left alone with Rachie in the dining-room.

The brother and sister had not the spirit to repair to the study this night, though Mrs. Baillie had taken the precaution to rake out the last embers of the fire from the grate in the family sitting-room, while the night was settling down piercingly cold.

Rachie was stitching at Dorcas work, the minister had let his head fall on his hand, and suffered himself to lapse into a gloomy silence. His sister could not bear to leave him to himself, but as the clock struck eleven she began to gather her work together.

'My mother will not be pleased if we sit up longer, wasting licht, since you are not studying, Wat,' she said in a pleading tone.

'Who said I was not studying?' he asked, recovering himself with a laugh which was not very joyous, 'the hardest lesson to study—a man's own failure, such a contemptible failure too. But it must be profitable; the contrite heart will be accepted in the day of small things as in that of great—don't you think so, Rachie? A straw may show how the wind blows—a straw has shown that I was careless, self-confident, and, as my mother says, light in the head.'

'Oh, Wat!' remonstrated Rachie—but as she spoke there came a rap at the front door, which sounded startlingly loud in the stillness of the house, for Mrs. Baillie's unflagging feet and voice were at rest for the next seven hours, and 'Sairey' was at liberty to sleep soundly on her chaff bed. It was a quick, stumbling rap, as of one eager to be heard and answered. It was also uncertain and tremulous in the application, like the rap of a person whose mind was disturbed and his purpose uncertain.

'What's that?' cried Rachie in a scared voice, as if it could be anything else than a rap, or as if thieves announced their entrance by a previous summons for admission.

'Somebody wanting me,' cried Wat, beginning to look brisk and hopeful again, as if there was the height of refreshment in the very idea of being wanted. 'It is well that I am of use yet. Stay where you are for a moment, Rachie, in case it be an errand for some poor sick body, with help needed instantly that they could not get elsewhere. I'll open the door, and take the messenger into the study. If I do not come back in five minutes go to your bed. I may have to turn out, for, you know, it may be a poor soul on the verge of another world, fain to be spoken for to his Maker and Father—as if that were wanted—and to have another word of consolation and encouragement; or his friends may be fain for him. In that case I'll lock the door, take the key, and let myself in.'

Wat went. Rachie heard him open the door, and apparently without waiting to hold more than a word of communication with the messenger, proceed to conduct the person to his study.

The next moment Wat came back as if he

had seen a ghost, for the colour of his own face was the gray of ashes. But he knew what he was about, for he closed the door behind him, and spoke in a whisper. 'Rachie, it is Miss Bruce Kirkpatrick. She has come the whole mirk road alone, in her slippers, with nothing but a rag of a handkerchief tied over her head. Hoar frost or sleet is falling, for her hair is powdered white, and her feet are soaking. She will get her death of cold. For God's sake make up the fire, give me the brandy, bring a change of clothes, and come to her immediately.'

'Miss Bruce—the nicht—at this hour—her lane!' cried Rachie, in a succession of gasps. 'Oh, Wat! what brings her here? She'll be your destruction, the destruction o' ye baith.'

'Whisht, whisht, woman! I cannot tell what brings her, and I cannot stop to ask. I'm afraid she has run away from Birkencraig.

Oh! make haste, Rachie, to succour her, for she is entitled to the best we have to give.'

Rachie was not so sure of that till she saw the wild-looking, dripping figure of the poor girl, whom she too had admired from a distance in the past as 'bonnie petted little Miss Bruce.'

Neither Rachie nor even Wat ever knew exactly what drove Bruce to the desperate step she took. She had come home from her banishment some time before Claud's release, and there had been an apparent reconciliation between them. She had gone with her sisters to visit him, and the sight of her brother in a gaol—however the situation might be glossed over, for an act to which she had given provocation—had completely overcome her proud, independent spirit, and the resentment she had been cherishing. She sobbed on Claud's shoulder, and begged him to forgive her, as if she alone had been in fault; while Claud suffered the embrace and granted the prayer for pardon as if they were his due.

But when Claud came home in triumph the tables were turned, and another temper was roused in the girl. She bethought herself of all the exposure he had brought on her, all the blame, humiliation, and ridicule she had been forced to undergo, and the unacknowledged, unrepented-of injury he had done her in his frantic passion rankled in her mind.

The elder Misses Kirkpatrick, in their lamentable supineness, had permitted Lord Sandy, and some other equally undesirable associates of Claud's, to assist at his homecoming, which was as much as to say that the festival was let degenerate into an orgy long before midnight. After most of the guests were gone, Claud, worn out with fatigue and excitement, and no longer fit for ladies' society, or for any other company, in an evil moment came across his young sister. He was not so lost to what was passing around him as to fail to see her usual indignant protest at the state he was in, and the companions who had reduced him to it. In his opinion she was now the last person in the world entitled to take such ground. He implied as much in a speech in which the taunt addressed to her was neither delicate nor veiled.

She answered sharply and quitted the room.

He followed her, and then the furious ill-conditioned lad, incapable of self-mastery or even common consideration of what he was about, committed some outrage which she would never repeat. He might have struck her an unmanly blow, he might merely have turned the key in the door of the room she had entered, with a loud remark that she was not fit to be trusted, and that it would be more like the thing if it were she and not he who was locked up.

Whatever he did, it was the last straw which broke the camel's back. The galling insult, which made all that had gone before it utterly unbearable, drove her into open revolt.

The room was an old school-room on the ground-floor; she had often before leapt out of the window in sport in day-light; she did it now in earnest, under cloud of night, when the rest of the household were assembled elsewhere.

For the moment Bruce was almost as reckless as Claud. She did not care what became of her, so that she escaped from farther cruel wrong at his hands.

Finding herself in the wet and darkness of an inclement night, she hardly knew where to turn, but half instinctively she took the familiar road to the manse, and traversed it still more aggrieved by the unwonted exposure which she had brought on herself. She was in a measure scared by it, and rendered wilder and more distraught. But she was not prevented from accomplishing the walk along the lonely road where still she might have been met, and whether recognised or not, stopped, assailed, insulted. She told herself, in her hot young blood and her ignorance, that she was fleeing from worse insult, and she was not hindered from making the only appeal which entered her head. The way appeared interminable, but it came to an end at last.

'Mr. Baillie,' she said distinctly, though her teeth were chattering and she was shaking like a leaf from head to foot,' 'will you take me in, and give me shelter to-night, and I will go away to-morrow and never trouble you or any other body more?' She addressed Rachie much in the same strain, calling her simply by her christian name, as Bruce had not been accustomed to do. 'Rachie, will you find a place for me and help me to get warm again, for I am perishing with cold? I think I never knew before what cold meant. Will you take me into your room or let me sit by the " happed " kitchen fire? I don't mind, and I'll go away as soon as it is light, and not put anybody about more than I can help.'

There was little sleep for Wat Baillie and his sister that night, though the deprivation was made up to one of them by the rapid growth of a dream of delight, contending successfully with a waking crowd of anxieties and cares. As for the cause of the sleeplessness, after she had been warmed and comforted in her body, she soon sank into the ready slumber of youth, and the combined exhaustion of extreme agitation and fatigue, for she had run rather than walked the distance.

So far as Wat could discover, she had formed no plan for the future beyond a vague vehement persuasion that she would die or suffer anything rather than go back to her brother's house, granting that he would take her in and not turn her from the door. She supposed, in an indefinite way, with the hazy half-sanguineness, half-despair of youth, some place would be found for her. She did not speak of her more distant relations, since she knew they had been displeased with her before as the cause of so much trouble; and she might well guess, even in the whirl and distraction of her ideas, that this fresh scandal and defiance would raise them all up in arms against her.

Wat had made his plans before morning, and imparted them to Rachie, who, for that matter, acquiesced in them, with many doubts and fears, sorely exercised for her beloved brother. It was as well that he was prepared, for the moment he came down from his room, he was hailed by his mother, who, to his surprise, prepared to sit down to breakfast in her bonnet and shawl, while his father wore his Sunday clothes.

Of course Mrs. Baillie knew of the arrival during the previous night, and she was not going to waste a moment in expressing her opinion of it.

'Are you bound for a journey, mother?' asked Wat, trying to speak as lightly and indifferently as possible.

'Ay, Wat, that am I,' she answered emphatically. 'It is high time I should be taking my foot in my hand. I cannot hinder sic on-goings as have taken place, and are a shame to a manse as they will be a by-word in the parish, but I can manifest they were with no will o' mine.'

'Mother,' he said, ' you had better wait for an explanation.'

'It doesna' behove me to wait, lad, and the thing bodes of no explanation. Na, na, you ha'e gotten another mistress for your manse, and I'm no wanted. Gin she had come a wise-like gate, at a proper time, and been a fit wife for you, I would ha'e made her welcome, and bidden still and learned her how to guide your house, and no bring you to ruin, as so mony men are brocht. But I'll stay for no gude-daughter—leddy or no leddy—it's an unco unleddy-like trick, who comes linkin' in the dark o' her ain accord, though I dinna misdoubt she got plenty o' encouragement; and it was a' plotted and schemed between you beforehand.'

'You are completely mistaken,' exclaimed Wat, whose colour had been rising to a deep glow, while his tongue was tied by the flow of words addressed to him.

'But ony way,' Mrs. Baillie rushed on in her charge, not to be silenced for a moment, 'she's thrown herself at a man's heid and ta'en refuge in his hoose like an ill-doer that dreaded waur wyte would fa' upon her.'

'This is not to be permitted, even from you,' protested Wat. starting up.

'And wha'll stop me?' demanded Mrs. Baillie, proceeding in a fine vein of irony. 'Permitted quo' he? Puir man, it will be a wonder gin he's permitted to keep his kirk after decoying a young leddy to break loose from her friends, and rin to him.'

'Mother, once for all, will you allow me to explain?'

'Explain awa', Wat, but words will no mend deeds.'

'If it is the presence of Miss Bruce Kirkpatrick in the house to which you object,' began Wat with an unconscious assumption of his stately manner, 'I grant you that is undesirable under present circumstances, but it will soon come to an end. She is to set out after breakfast with Rachie.'

'And where are they gaun'?' interrupted Mrs. Baillie with inflated nostrils, 'and what for am I no to be consulted about Rachie's gaun'? I daur her to gang ony gate without my knowledge and leave. I forbid her to steer a step—a fell-like minister you are, Wat Bilie wi' a' your troke o' duty, and morals, and warks, first to entice a lassie and back her against her brother and sisters—though I'm no sayin' the scripter demands honour for them—and syne to put up Rachie to deceit and insubordination.'

'Mother,' said Wat, ' it is the one favour I ask from you, and if you refuse it, I do not hesitate to say I will never ask another. Rachie is only to accompany Miss Bruce Kirkpatrick three hours' journey by the train to the house of my old friend and principal Dr. Rattray. He is a respected minister of the Church of Scotland, the esteemed head of a college—you yourself were proud when he came to preach for me and said *that* was something like preaching. You know his house was a second home to me when I was at college, and Mrs. Rattray was a second mother. I have given Rachie a letter to the Doctor, and Mrs. Rattray will not refuse to take in my sister and Miss Bruce Kirkpatrick for my sake. Now, have you anything to say against such a step? Will it compromise Rachie? or am I the man to ask her to do anything that could go against the grain with her, or reasonably offend you?'

In spite of herself, Mrs. Baillie was taken aback by the resolute statement, but she was not inclined to show how far she was impressed, or to give in more than she could avoid, though Wat's solemn passionate words about the one favour he would ask from her, had their effect. 'And you'll be to follow the lasses a' in gude time,' she said with a little accent of derision; 'and there will be a braw weddin' ower in Edinburgh, if Dr. and Mrs. Rattray are sic fules as to lend themselves to white-wash a bad job.

'That is as it may be. That is for another person to decide,' said Wat, keeping his temper, and speaking firmly, though again the tell-tale colour rose high in his face. He had carried his point so far that Mrs. Baillie did not forbid Rachie to go on her brother's errand, but neither would their mother defer her own and her husband's abrupt departure. She said she had sent out to Lowrie who had a message to the town that morning, to bid Geordie Cleghorn fetch her box, and it would be the waste of a hire for her to change her mind which besides she saw no sufficient cause for doing. She was going to her cousin's at the other side of Whinny Loan, she had got many a bidding— and she could look about her and settle what was to become of her and Tammas afterwards. They were up in years, and would not need the little they wanted long. Their son, for whom they had fought a battle in their prime, who had his kirk and his manse and all his orders and was about to intermarry with the gentry, could not have the face to let them starve, she could lippen to him for that, but these newfangled notions of what was right were not for her, and her presence was not desirable in the changes which were coming.

Wat could not contradict her, though his heart was sore at her desertion of him. He could only slip one of the two five-pound notes which were in the house into his father's hand, and volunteer to come and see the couple in the course of the week.

The nest was flown where the imperious old bird and her submissive mate were concerned, and Bruce had only to encounter Rachie and her brother when she came down. The girl was shy with a trepidation that was foreign to her and yet was winning in her.

But in the middle of her distress there was still an evident spice of relish for the excitement of a strange adventure, enough to prove that she scarcely realised to this moment, the grave consequences of what she had done in a fit of anger and rashness. Here also all the forethought and foreboding, 'the heavier end of the string,' as they say in Scotland, was left for Wat to carry.

He told her what he proposed she should do as soon as they were alone together; and while she looked at him questioningly, doubtfully, with her brown eyes alight, and her colour and breath coming and going fast in a tumult of contradictory feelings, he added a few words which could not be mistaken. 'I am sending you away from the manse, because it seems best for you to anticipate idle gossip. But it rests with yourself whether you will not soon return and stay here for the rest of your days as the honoured mistress of the house, so far as its master can heap honour upon you, as his dear wife.'

'Oh, I did not mean that,' she said piteously, her colour coming and going worse than ever.

'I know,' he said, gently; 'and I would not

hurry you if it could be helped; I am sure you believe that. I would not take advantage of your position, if I were convinced you had an insuperable objection to the end I am proposing, which I am mad enough to think is the most natural, the wisest, and best end after all, though you did not mean it. Your family will be offended, and if I had not good reason to suppose they were so already, beyond the hope of reconciliation, it would be my duty to try, first to heal the breach, which I am satisfied is no longer susceptible of healing. I fancy I, too, did not dare to mean this end in the beginning, still, even in the ordinary course of events, we might have come to think of it—you don't deny it—Bruce, my dear love,' cried Wat, carried away by the dazzling vision of a bright, fair, loving wife, the very 'little Miss Bruce' of the past, to share his manse and his life. 'Of course I know I am not your equal; you are stooping to me—you will have to resign many things, put up with many things. You will have to make allowance for my ways.'

She interrupted him quickly, with eyes which began to stream. 'Wat Baillie, you are the best man I ever knew. The life you have led is as much higher than what my life has been as the sky is above the earth. That is a good reason for thinking I ought to refuse you, though I do not know where to turn, or what to do. If you had been like any other man, you would have let me feel that I had not only put myself in your power, but left you without any other choice save to make me this offer—that is another good reason for me to decline it. Oh, I wish you would suffer me to go, and not care about me. If you only guessed how ashamed I am,' covering her face with her hands.

'Ashamed!' he cried, drawing them down, 'of what I am so proud—that you could still trust me, though, like the lout I am, I affronted you once—I was so left to myself as to take by a rude liberty, what has become mine by a dear right.'

CHAPTER XIII.

THE END OF THE HONEYMOON.

It all happened very much as Wat had proposed. The Rattrays, a rather high-bred, benevolent old couple, who had already been surprised, sorry, and, in spite of themselves, diverted at the scrape in which their old pupil and *protégé* had found himself, were again electrified by the consequences. 'Wonders will never cease,' cried the lively old lady. ' To think of a minister of the respectable old Kirk, that great heavy, steady Wat Baillie, whom you used to call your right hand, running away with a lassie, or rather of a lassie of our class running away with him! I cannot help thinking she must have a fine spirit, for he would be hard to drag along by her apron-string.'

The pair did not refuse to lend Wat the countenance he craved, in the most decorous mode he could devise, for extricating Bruce and himself from their difficulty. The Rattrays were all the more won over by their aristocratic bias, which laid it upon them, as a positive obligation, to shelter Bruce Kirkpatrick from the punishment of her imprudence. The same proclivity inclined them to be charmed with her, as if she were the fittest wife for a soberminded minister, the mistress of a manse whose management of its narrow means would not ruin her husband, which Wat's mother had been in the habit of assuming was the ordinary work of wives.

Fortunately for all concerned, Bruce Kirkpatrick had run away from her brother and sisters, and not from her father and mother, else the Church might have had something to say to Wat's share in the escapade. But the distinction pointed out made a great difference in the eyes of even the strictest formulators of censures. To quote Mrs. Baillie again, there was no scripture command to honour—in the sense of to obey—a brother or a sister. When the subsequent marriage ceremony was performed with all the proper rites, including the 'crying' three times in the kirk, and the pronouncing of the blessing of the Kirk by the voice of an ordained minister, not John Knox in the flesh could have found any flaw in the performance.

One thing which he could have hardly hoped for, was a great relief for the present to Wat. The two elder Misses Kirkpatrick—not to say Claud—were so moved by the extent of Bruce's wrong-doing—her frantic revolt, withdrawal in future from their authority and establishment under their very eyes in the manse of Birkenbarns as the wife of the parish minister Muckle Wat Baillie, son of the old grieve at Rintoul, that the whole family quitted Birkencraig, as they had not done for a period of years, and repaired to a popular watering-place, there to spend the spring and early summer, on the plea of the benefit to Claude's health. What was to be acted on their return—whether they were to cut young Mrs. Baillie dead, and the manse and one of the principal heritors' houses were to present to the parish the unedifying spectacle of permanent family strife and estrangement, or whether a hollow peace and reconciliation were to be patched up between the ladies, remained among the dubious questions of the future. In the meanwhile, there was no doubt Wat's marriage brought about his partial restoration to favour in the eyes of the disaffected members of the community. Certainly there were many still hostile and disposed to talk coldly of bad examples. But, on the other hand, there was enough romance left in the world, both among high and low, for other recusants—above all the comparatively neutral—to be softened by the agreeable sight of the winsome, bonnie young brides. She appeared constantly in the minister's pew in church, and frequently by Wat Baillie's side in his walks on his 'ministerial visitations,' with or without poor Rachie, who had dwindled away into an inferior satellite.

Not only the elders—including the Laird of Murniepae—who had come and conferred with Wat on his indiscretion, now to a man congratulated him on his marriage, and arrived with their wives and daughters to call for young Mrs. Baillie; the fancies of the old and the young of all ranks were caught by Bruce as they had never been before. The old among the orthodox, evangelical poor were still disposed to deny her the supernatural gift of grace, they were even tempted to distrust their minister in this indispensable quality—the absence of which would be a sore lack in his office, while they magnanimously hoped the defect would be supplied in time. Till then, these competent judges were content to be benefited and cheered by the benefactions and notice so much more liberal and kindly than in old Mrs. Baillie's day, of the couple whom the Scotch pharisees held as *suspects*—suspected of latitudinarianism, erastianism, and any number of isms.

The young of the same class made no bones of bestowing their favour, but enjoyed to the full the bright smile, sweet voice, and easy merry words of the pretty young lady, once Miss Bruce Kirkpatrick. They had always known her, and they at least had not disliked her, but she came more among them, and was nearer to them now. She helped the minister to distribute the school prizes, and she assisted Miss Rachie to marshal and entertain the scholars, big and small, at their summer feast.

People took a fond pride in remembering later—and the more indulgent of the old wives were fain to ascribe the fact in the end to the first sprouts of that free grace they were so wary in according to Bruce—how she tried to suit herself to her altered circumstances, how the young wife strove to render herself acceptable to her husband's parishioners, so as to prove herself a help and no longer a hindrance to him. She was so frank and unaffected in her gentle breeding, that though she had not hitherto been popular in her own rank, it was not hard for her to make a good impression under fresh auspices on both old and young, while the minister was enchanted by the golden opinions she was winning. Still, she had her prejudices, and she must have stifled them to sit down so readily in inferior places and at inferior boards, to walk where she was wont to ride or drive, as a rule to drink tea with farmers and their wives or the household circles in neighbouring manses, instead of dining with lords and lairds and their ladies, attending christenings and comings of age in high places, and dancing at county balls. She must have put force on herself to be satisfied with the homely economy at the manse—in which she had the sense to let Rachie initiate her, and to go with Wat to see his mother and father in their new character as her mother and father—to whom she owed duty and service, which were not made less difficult by Mrs. Baillie's grudging sour manner of accepting them, so far removed from Mary and Lily Kirkpatrick's good-natured graciousness. Every body in the parish admitted her marriage must have made a great change to young Mrs. Baillie, and most people added she accommodated herself to it bravely and sweetly—a proof of that good and honest heart which had lain neglected and choked by a false over-growth in Bruce Kirkpatrick. For one must remember that her worthy wifely efforts had not the impelling motive and immediate reward of a passionate attachment to Wat Baillie. Love had only been dawning between the couple, and the coy indications of the coming day will not, under whatever press of circumstances, pass in a bound to the strong light and heat of noon. As it was, Wat had gone considerably in advance of Bruce in this, as in most other schools. Her sentiments for him when she married him were largely made up of genuine reverence, hearty contrition and deep unfeigned gratitude—no bad soil for love, but not love any more than the nourishment is the growth it produces.

Even Rachie had to allow Bruce did her best, did well in the middle of the devoted sister's sharp struggle at giving up the first place in Wat's regard, with the additional jealous tortured sense that what she had cherished as the highest earthly good was lightly held by the woman who had gained the prize without seeking for it, and without any true sense of its real value. Yet what Rachie reluctantly owned then, she would have vouched for with her heart's blood, before she was many months older.

It might have been partly from the absence of passionate love for her husband, as well as from the magnanimity of the nobler sort of pride, that Bruce insisted the brother and sister should continue together the studies in which they took such delight, but in which she could not join.

At first she had said with cheerful humility, she would be their pupil; but with all the will in the world on Wat's side, it was found this could not be, since there were not the elements of a student or scholar in any Kirkpatrick. Bruce was the readiest to own and submit to the truth. She declared herself content to be left behind, like many a wife in this region, and to pursue her own devices as she had been accustomed to do, during the time Wat and Rachie spent over their books. It did not follow from this that poor Bruce, who was very human and fallible, failed to feel a little hurt and resentful when her companions took her at her word, in complete unconsciousness, so far as Wat was concerned, and only ruefully on Rachie's side, when she recollected herself and bethought her of whose rights she was invading, and what was most becoming in these later days.

But in the very exuberance of Wat's satisfaction in his honeymoon—for he was an easily pleased, unassuming, unexacting fellow, who had been accustomed to hard lines under his mother—he turned sometimes in the joy of his heart, with renewed zest, to the chief of his old earthly sources of happiness and became engrossed with it for the moment—almost to the exclusion of later and still more heartfelt interests. How should he guess that Bruce felt lonely or sad when she had only been left to herself for half an evening, and when she was so much mistress of the situation as to refrain from giving the slightest sign of weariness or chagrin —so far from that, she would be at her gayest, almost startlingly gay afterwards? And Wat was too sincere and slow in some respects to draw any save the most agreeable inference from the incessant talk, banter, and laughter.

But Bruce gradually vacated the study more and more to the brother and sister. She was wont to take refuge from this and the other tolerably rough rubs of her early married life, in the manse-garden, or on the Craig. She would climb the last surreptitiously in order to wander aimlessly among the blaeberries and heather, or to sit and gaze wistfully at the chimneys of Birkencraig bereft of its owners.

Bruce had always been fond of the manse-garden, so different from the formal beds at Birkencraig and destitute of a despot of a gardener. For Lowrie did as she bade him, for a wonder, without venturing to interfere with her will and pleasure. She began to grow an enthusiastic gardener in her own person, displaying the same ability in the floral art that she had shown in the profession of nursing. She projected a half-natural terrace grown over with rock plants, and a new walk shaded by tufts of bracken imported from the Craig and intermingled with laurel bushes, long kept up in memory of those days. She first induced Wat to lend her his strong back and lengthy arms, telling him that she would improve his hands, and then appointed him her assistant and worked him hard under her orders to the simple-minded giant's high gratification. She was not like Charlotte Lucas in 'Pride and Prejudice,' who encouraged her clerical husband in gardening ostensibly for the sake of his health, really to get rid, for hours every day, of the heavy drag of his society. The minister and his wife at Birkenbarns gardened a great deal together, like Adam and Eve, that summer, and about the happiest of the swiftly passing hours were thus spent.

Among the lost privileges of her old state which Bruce regretted was her riding. She had been a good rider as well as walker, but she had not conceived, till riding failed her, how she would crave a variety of exercise, and how unmixed walking would become tame and tiresome. One afternoon Bruce had gone with Rachie to pay a visit to the farm-house of Mr. Dunlop, Wat's Elder, at the Bow of Birkenbarns, where Wat was to follow his wife and sister. Then Bruce could not resist the temptation to an impromptu ride suggested to her in the course of some remarks made to her by her host, who asked her advice on a question troubling him. He and she had fraternised from the first, when Mrs. Wat had gladly hailed him as an old acquaintance of the hunting-field. He told her he had been empowered by the widow of his late laird to buy a riding horse at the June market, for the use of her youngest daughter. He had made the purchase but had not sent the beast home, as he was a good deal exercised in his mind by doubts of the animal's perfect steadiness and docility in the hands of a lady—an inexperienced rider.

'Oh, will you let me try her, Mr. Dunlop?' begged Bruce with eager coaxing. 'You know I am not a bad rider, and I think I could tell what would suit Alice Crawford. Never mind a habit, let me go as I am and have a good gallop round the Lea,' referring to the great pasture meadow in which the house stood. 'Do let me go before tea, I shall eat twice as many of Mrs. Dunlop's scones if you will only give your consent.'

'But what would the minister say,' remonstrated the smiling, and on this occasion not contentious, but only too-yielding guardian of the mare, 'supposing you should get a fling and break your bones?'

'Suppose nothing so insulting to my horsemanship—you who have seen me follow the hounds with—with Mr. Kirkpatrick for the better part of the day, when the fences were not too stiff, or the ditches too wide. Of course I could not pretend to such a leap as carried you in, first of the field, at the King's Crook— don't you remember, Mr. Dunlop?'

Didn't he remember? and wasn't he flattered by his minister's wife—as fine a young lady as ever lived, recalling—what none there save he and she could recall—to his glory as a sportsman, though that was but a worldly vanity when men looked at it in a serious light. He was prepared to do her almost any favour, however, after that speech.

Rachie objected, but though Bruce, as everybody agreed, behaved well to Rachie, the young matron did not see herself called upon to submit to her unmarried sister-in-law's control in what was not Rachie's province, in what, for that matter, she was quite unversed, since Rachie Baillie was of a timid disposition, in contrast to her size, and had not mounted a horse—not even a cart-horse, in her whole life.

Besides, poor Rachie, whose learning did not prevent her from being unrefined, had unconsciously provoked the young lady, her sister-in-law, several times that afternoon, by the unvarnished expression of a country dressmaker's opinions, and the unhesitating practice of her homely habits. Bruce was neither hypercritical nor hypocritical, but she was still sufficiently small to allow herself to be offended by trifles light as air. She had asked herself what call had Rachie to descant like a professional on the 'sit,' and the 'hang,' the width of the 'sey,' and the length of the 'tail' of Mrs. Dunlop's children's dresses; or to put pins in her mouth; or to sleek her hair in a fashion with which Bruce was totally unacquainted? Young Mrs. Baillie had grown irritable and restive under those pin-pricks, though she had possessed the good taste and good feeling to keep her fastidiousness and fault-finding spirit to herself. All the same, though the two causes seem to have no necessary connection, the grains of offence she had received did not dispose her the more to defer to Rachie's remonstrance against riding a strange horse unattended. For Bruce had scouted Mr. Dunlop's halting proposal, that he should take out his horse and accompany her. 'Certainly not, Mr. Dunlop; to give all that trouble for a gallop round the Lea, when I have followed the hounds for the better part of a day,' she cried in chagrin. And somehow he thought it would look foolish, she might take it as presumption in him, though she was only the minister's wife now, and was to drink tea with his good wife and himself, the minister and Rachie Baillie, the old Rintoul dress-maker, on something like terms of equality, which might very well be, when he was one of the leading Elders of the parish. Still he could not altogether forget that on that day at the King's Crook, to which she had alluded, she had been closely attended for the entire morning—there had been some mistaken word of her marriage with the lad in consequence— by the son of the master of the fox hounds, the finest sprig of quality in the field. There was no reasonable apology for the farmer's escort. It was an altogether different matter for a good rider like Mrs. Wat Baillie, and a school-girl like Miss Alice Crawford, to mount the mare, while Mrs. Baillie's opinion was worth having, and she could not give it till she tried the animal

The whole family party accompanied Bruce to the farm-house door, after she had first tied on her hat to shade her eyes, and drawn on her gauntlets lest the creature should tug at the bridle. She looked with sparkling eyes at the handsome bay, and was more covetous than critical.

'Oh, she is bonnie!' she cried enthusiastically; then proceeded to praise with effusion the horse's size, shape, coat, head, and tail. Finally Bruce confidently announced that she would find no difficulty in riding the mare, though it was not certain that she would do for Alice Crawford.

The rider was suffered to start alone, looking blythe and very bonnie herself, and turning to smile and nod as she set off with no further demonstration from the high-spirited horse than a little toss of the head and quiver of the shoulders.

There was no question the mare had found her mistress, and Mrs. Baillie could manage her though the horse had increased her speed, and was going like the wind when she passed Wat Baillie walking leisurely along the path through the pasture. But the horsewoman was flying along at her ease, full of restrained power, quite capable of enjoying the joke of the blank surprise of her husband.

There was a corner to be taken, with a projecting elder-bush round which Bruce turned sharply. The farmer who had been watching the vanishing rider, thought of the manner in which both root and branches of this bush extended round the corner, with the first twinge of anxiety, when he saw how near she had ridden on this side. He walked quickly in the direction of the bush, but did not overtake Wat Baillie, who had turned, and, somewhat to the amusement of the more distant group at the door, began to hurry after his wife. It was therefore Wat who first passed the screen which the elder formed, and saw right in front of him a woman's figure in a heap on the grass, and still farther in advance a riderless horse galloping more wildly than ever.

In the few seconds it took him to reach her, he had begun to thank God she had fallen among the meadow grass, and was probably not much hurt, though she lay so still. But when he came nearer to her he saw another thing that made his blood run cold again. It was the long sharp spur of the root—like one of the whale's jaw-bones which an eccentric fancy had placed, in the room of pillars, at the entrance into this very field. The treacherous root, half-hidden in the grass, had escaped the eyes of both horse and woman. It was the root which had caught the mare's hoofs when she was at the top of her speed, and without bringing her down, caused her to stumble suddenly and heavily. It was across the root that Bruce lay.

But God was merciful. As there was no outward injury, beyond her stunned condition, to be seen at a glance, there might still be no grievous harm done.

There was plenty of assistance, and no lack of sympathy at hand. Mr. Dunlop kept telling his minister, as they carried the lifeless-looking figure back to the house, to keep up his heart; Mrs. Dunlop would have a bed prepared, and restoratives ready before they could reach the house; he or one of his men would ride and fetch the doctor in less than half-an-hour; the speaker had often seen worse accidents in the hunting-field with no mischief to speak of.

But Wat could not resist the impression—from the very fervour of the well-meant, kindly-uttered assurances—that Mr. Dunlop held there was great necessity for keeping up their hearts from the moment he saw where and how the accident had happened.

The women undressed Bruce and laid her on the bed before she moved or spoke, and even then, while the minister's heart leapt up at the light of her eyes and the sound of her voice again, she was half stupefied still. She did not know where she was, who was beside her, or what had happened to her, though she moaned by fits and starts as if she were in pain and made little convulsive movements, as if she would be restless were she able to throw her self about.

But full intelligence came back before the doctor arrived, and then Bruce comforted some of her listeners by saying she was not in pain— at least not in much—only very uncomfortable she must admit, in spite of all they had been so good as to do for her, and oddly tired and helpless, she supposed she was sick from the blow or the shock. 'It was not Mr. Dunlop's or Rachie's fault,' were the first words which were coherently though faintly spoken to Wat. 'She was against my going, and I must say I distrusted her eyes—the mare's eyes—but I longed so for one good gallop again, and I thought just round the Lea there could be no great risk. Wat, bid them look after the mare—she *is* a fine horse, though she will never do for Alice Crawford. But she was not vicious, you know, just keen to be off, and she could not help herself, with that horrid tree-root. Tell Mr. Dunlop he ought to have it chopped off, or sawn asunder, or something—better the bush be spoilt than people hurt; why, somebody might be killed there one day.'

'Hush, my dear, hush!' implored Wat, with a sword going through his heart; 'you must not speak so much till the doctor sees you.'

The doctor came at last and examined his patient carefully without eliciting a louder moan from her. She was able to make a joke to him on their old ambulance class, and he answered it with another joke; but his face fell the moment he left the room, and Wat's heart, which had risen like a feather within the last three or four minutes, fell again with the density of lead.

'Mr. Baillie, I am sorry to say your wife has met with a bad—a very bad accident,' said the medical man, so accustomed to make painful communications that he could deliver this with composure; yet he was so far from destitute of fellow-feeling that the matter-of-fact brevity of the sentence was simply the result of his own instinctive recoil from the distress he was causing and the further misery he knew to be in store for his listener.

'Is she in danger?' inquired Wat in the same quiet manner, though surges were ringing in his ears, and his own voice sounded to him like that of another person speaking at an immeasurable distance.

'Poor chap,' the doctor was saying to himself, 'he will have need of the consolations he accustomed to administer to other people—before all is ended. That fine girl, so clever at picking up the hints of my trade, and she ran away with him not four months since!' He said aloud, 'I am greatly afraid she is in danger; I should recommend you to have further advice without delay.'

Telegrams were written and farther messengers sent here and there, regardless of trouble or cost, while Bruce lay and dosed with only that involuntary moaning and twitching to disturb her sleep. She woke up to smile a little at being put at once on invalid's fare. 'I was to have eaten so many of Mrs. Dunlop's scones—don't you remember? and now I am only to have slops—it is very hard.' To the uninitiated it looked as if she were not doing badly at all, but for what she herself considered her inexplicable uselessness and weakness, while the last became less prominent after fever began to rise and to furnish her with artificial strength.

Wat had telegraphed to Dr. Rattray, who had helped him before at another pinch, to send through the foremost medical man in the capital to pronounce Bruce's doom as it proved. For he had no more comfortable words for Wat than, 'I regret I can say no more than that while there is life there is hope. The case is as bad as it can well be.' Then he added some technical words as to the fatal injury to the spine which would have been incomprehensible to Wat, with all his learning, at the best of times, and was now part of an unknown tongue.

'Cease ye from man whose breath is in his nostrils.' Put not your trust in him though he were a prince ruling with a rod of iron, far less a simple physician, the teacher of a science which—as all honest men admit—the long centuries have not been able to bring beyond the babble of infancy.

But surely there is help still in the Maker of the universe, with whom are the issues of life and death. He was Wat's God and could not destroy the happiness He had given. He could not take from His servant, by a stroke the treasure he had hardly grasped. Alas! Wat knew better. He was not a minister for nothing. One of his principal duties was to visit the sick and bereaved, to break, with holy words of faith and submission, the tidings of many an unlooked-for disaster, to incredulous and wailing sufferers. What was he that he should count himself exempted from the common lot, even from an exceptionally hard lot? Had not Wat often taught the strange sad mystery that whom the Lord loved He chastened, and scourged every son whom He received? It belonged to the yoke which in another sense was easy, that Wat should pass over the red-hot ploughshares and the sharp goads and harrows, if possible without a murmur. It was only fit that he too, though at an immeasurable distance from his Master, should be made perfect through suffering, that he might be able to help those who suffered. The spiritual physician was called on to heal himself of his deadly wound.

Wat made one last despairing effort at resistance. The doctors could not mean *that* by their long faces and gibberish. They only meant, and it was bad enough, that his Bruce, who was so young, lithe, and active, in whose light foot and perfect health he had rejoiced, was thenceforth to be a sickly cripple, never more to move without help from bed or couch. But he would give himself up to caring for and solacing her, since God had made her his first charge. He would surround her with every thing which the heart of woman in her melancholy position could desire, till she should almost cease to regret her deprivations. But what was the meaning of that lifelessness creeping on and on, of the stillness of the once animated body which no feverish unrest could affect? He could not deceive himself for a minute; and must he also undeceive Bruce, who, because of a little temporary ease, and the fever which while consuming her vital force was lending her a false and fleeting life, talked cheerfully at intervals of her removal home and her subsequent recovery? It was difficult for the most despondent and the best informed as to her state, not to believe the person most concerned in it. And who was to tell what might be an untruth after all, to one from whom God had withheld the knowledge—if it were knowledge—of the great change, near at hand, with which she had so much to do?'

But when Wat returned to his wife, after his interview with the two doctors, the smile had faded from her lips, and he saw that her eyes were startled and grave with anxiety and earnestness. 'Shall I not go back to the manse, Wat?' she asked faintly.

'They say not, Brucie,' he answered in a choked voice, unconsciously using the tender child's name, which her people had given her long ago. 'But they may be wrong, and if not, you are going to a better place, where I hope and pray to follow you soon.'

She was dumb under the awfulness of the information, only her great solemn eyes broke his heart by the look which seemed to say, 'Oh, Wat Baillie, can you do no more than they can for me?'

Then Wat girded himself to do what was left to him—his best while his heart was like stone in his breast. If it could serve her, he must not fail her. He began to read and speak the words he had often read and spoken to other voyagers on the verge of the shoreless sea. They had sounded living words before, though they were like dead words to him to-day, and he could hardly conceive it was himself who was reading and praying, it was so much like a perfect stranger rehearsing once again a tale that had been often told. It was the most cruel grief, at the core of his grief—too sharp to be borne long, while faith in Heaven—the last boon of the wretched—lived on. Had his Master forsaken him in the hour of his bitter anguish, and left him to sink in the deep waters? or had he no Master? Was there no Heaven, only a material perishing world, while the life that was dearer to him than his own was ebbing swiftly away before his eyes, without any power on his part to retain it?

No, no. The blue heavens continued above the hapless couple, though clouds and darkness had come between. The everlasting arm was not shortened, the great right hand of Almighty truthfulness and mercy was not, could not be, closed. It was but the crushed, reeling creature, who even while he clung half mechanically to the last trusted stay, had ceased, not unnaturally, to feel the strong, gentle clasp. The ever-open ear of the Heavenly Father and Divine Elder Brother was not stopped to human groaning, though Wat Baillie had become deaf and blind, like a dead man before his time, in the sore trouble of his life.

The words which were half frozen on his lips, must have melted as they fell, and dropped softly like dew on the thirsting heart. There was nothing save peace in her face, or in anything she said afterwards, so long as she lingered. She muttered many a foolish wandering word in her growing weakness, but not one that he or she need have wished unspoken.

'Among adders! Did Muckle Wat save me from them, or did he bring me among them, and then smile and bid me not mind their hissing tongues, for he would keep them from doing me any harm, though he should take all the poison into his own veins?

'Only four months since our wedding-day at the dear old Rattrays, who have not visited us yet, and never will now. Only four months married—not long to get used to each other, and become all the world to each other; but I think we were growing fonder and fonder of each other every day. I called him "Wattie" the other morning, and reminded him that was what we called the ganders, and he laughed and said he did not care, any name from my lips was sweet—the silly old man! I was looking at him the night before last—no, the night before I met my death, after he had fallen asleep on the sofa, and I was proud of his big brow, and wondered I had ever seen anything wrong with his ears, or thought that other ears would have become him better. I hoped if I ever bore him a son, that the boy would be the image of his father. I kissed him without his knowing it. I meant to tell Wat I had taken back the stupid kiss he snatched from me long ago, which people made such a work about, so that it cost him dear.

'We might have been a marvel of married love, but I daresay it is better as it is, for the Kirkpatricks are not made for good husbands and wives. Self-indulgence is it? or pride under the garb of humility? or want of grace, as old Nanny at the toll used to say? I shall get it at last where I am going; there is sufficient for all wants yonder, since One is at the door who never grudged or stinted what He gave, and the minister says He will let me in, and put what I lack into my bosom good measure, pressed down and running over.

'I might not always have done my best here, I might have failed after all. I pined sometimes for wretched little things I should not have thought I would have wasted a sigh upon— silk gowns and lace handkerchiefs, a plate of Mattie's hare soup, or claret jelly handed to me by Nicol, some of the biscuits Lily feeds her dogs with; I believe I even missed afternoon visits and the excitement of a drive to Sauchope. Oh! What a weak wicked goose. I was angry with Rachie without a cause, and

I craved the ride for which I am paying with my life. I might have gone on getting angry and craving, paying higher and higher prices, and not discharging the debt alone, with innocent noble Wat Baillie made accountable for it. But now he has put down what was owing to the uttermost farthing. And they will see how he has suffered, and say he has been punished enough.

'Wat and Rachie will go back to their books and be taken up with them again, but they will not forget me. I am better off than the poor woman in the queer song Wat read to me once. How did it go?

> It killed her, the brute!
> On the stump of the willow tree;
> And only the baby wept
> For poor Lorraine Loree.

'Oh! there will be a great many people—far more than I deserve—sorry for me, Wat most of all and Claud next.' She startled her husband by looking up and speaking distinctly to him. 'Send for Mary and Lily and Claud, all of them, to come at once;' then she replied to the pained perplexity in his eyes. 'Do you think Claud will not come? Do you think he did not care for me? Oh! it is little you know though you are wise—but not with worldly wisdom, Wat Baillie. Why, Claud liked me better than anybody, save himself. He was prouder of me than of anything, unless perhaps his horses, which were never very good ones, poor boy, he was so taken in by Lord Sandy and the dealers God forgive them. Claud and I were as much together as you and Rachie when we were young; we did not read books, of course, but we sought birds' nests and harried them too, sometimes, I am sorry to say, and walked on stilts and put on false faces and rode—what rides we had together! Well, I did not hope to have Claud at the manse I must say, but I looked for the two others—some day. I was going to show off as a housekeeper to

Mary, and to cram Lily's hands with our roses and lilies, and give her the best of the little white bantam's brood. It is all to be different, but no doubt it is for the best, and I shall have Claud—you will see.' He saw—not she. The eyes of her body and her mind too were dark to all the sights of this life, though she was still alive, and the soul had not quitted its fair fragile tenement, when those who were summoned without ceremony and apology, for a last meeting in this world, with Claud among them, could not find it in their hearts to disobey that summons. Mary and Lily were weeping their soft eyes out, but Claud, as he bent with a haggard dry face, over his sister, only gave one great tearless sob.

'Mr. Baillie, I would give all the horses I have in my stables, ay, ten times over, that I had never let yon brute among them—that I had never suffered the poor young lady to mount her,' Mr. Dunlop protested sorrowfully to Wat on the evening of the day of Bruce's death.

'You could not help it,' said the widower in a dull, measured tone; 'she did not blame even the brute of a horse. She wished the mare to be valued and cared for.'

'Well, sir, if you do not wyte a man who would have gone a long road before he would willingly have hurt you or her to a hair of your heads, prove your goodness by not going back to the manse your lea' lone as I see you are preparing to do. Wait till Rachie your sister can accompany you. I am no great company for a scholar, but let me or any other of your Elders you like to pick out stay with you in your trial. We'll be proud to serve you. Murnipae was at College, and though he has no great gumption in a market, he may be another man among books.'

'Thanks, thanks, Dunlop, I'll not forget

your kindness, but believe me I'm better left alone,' the minister assured his friend wearily.

'They will see how you have suffered, and say you have been punished enough, just as she anticipated,' he told himself. 'But what can they do? They cannot bring her back. What do I care for them, except in common gratitude. Oh! Bruce, Bruce that was mine, that is mine through eternity, but I cannot hear you or see you, my darling, that was growing fonder and fonder of me. Little Miss Bruce, whom I had learned to love as I love my life, that I only clasped in my arms for four short summer months before the Master called her.'

There was a great gathering in Birkenbarns Kirk on the Sunday after Bruce had been buried in the minister's ground in the churchyard, to hear her funeral sermon. It was not preached by her husband. He sat conspicuous in his mourning among the hearers, as he had sat but yesterday, as it seemed, on his proclamation day, when the banns between him and Bruce Kirkpatrick were published to an interested world, arousing the congregation to one broad smile, and the embarrassed bridegroom to a hot blush. The preacher was a sympathising brother-minister in the Presbytery, himself a widower, who had lost, not long before, the companion of many years, the mother of his children. He spoke with feeling therefore, though he dealt in generalities, and was as often as not referring mentally to his own case, which was not quite parallel to that of his bereft brother.

But it was rather the occasion and the infectious sentiment of the crowd that came to commemorate the event, than any appropriate address or eloquent oration which was calculated to stir the people. There had not been such a gathering in the kirk since the day of Wat's ordination—many present thought of it—he among the rest. He recalled the bright young girl, the laird of Birkencraig's sister, who had given him her hand at the door with the cordial greeting, 'I am glad to see you, Mr. Baillie; I am glad to have been here to-day.' He thought of her when she surprised him, alone in the church, and in her girlish glee kept him in a state of mingled exasperation, alarm, and amusement, while she shook the keys in his face, through the window, from the ill-balanced tombstone and threatened to ring the kirk-bell and summon the parish to find him locked in, before he could stop her. He remembered the dark rainy night when the hurried rap had come to the door of the manse a bow-shot off, and he had opened it to discover her on the threshold come to him as her refuge and deliverer. And it was his destiny to sit there and know the sweet body to be lying in the dust till the morning of the resurrection, while he conned his Master's lesson of learning to say, 'Thy will be done.'

Not only were the Misses Kirkpatrick, in the crape and white cambric which they wore in keeping with the minister, in the family pew, Claud sat wan and worn in his late father's seat. Every once familiar face was at its old post, and was not likely to vanish with the day, for there was some pricking of conscience and an inclination to allay the little smart by a handsome atonement. The fulfilment of the penalty on Wat Baillie's part was amply acknowledged, and his last popularity was likely to be greater and more enduring than his first.

It would be a satisfaction to say, with the assurance which proofs give, that Bruce's death became new life to her brother. But so far as his career here might have witnessed to his amendment, the opportunity was not granted to him. In the winter of the same year a bad cold, ending in acute inflammation, cut short his few and evil days. At least the brother and sister whose love had worked each other, not weal but woe, in their deaths were not long divided.

Mary and Lily showed themselves all but inconsolable for this last loss. They proceeded to canonise their boy on the spot, and to speak of him for ever afterwards as one would refer to a departed saint.

To them Wat became as a son, and it was a sign how they got, by degrees, to appreciate and depend upon him in another relation from that which had originally existed between them, when towards the close of their lives the ladies would voluntarily and publicly admit the family connection which his marriage with Bruce had established, by speaking of him sometimes to their old friends as 'our brother the minister of Birkenbarns.'

Wat and Rachie live on together in the manse, and continue fast friends. They both grow more learned, and he especially more devout and charitable, so that he is frankly recognised to be the best, as well as the most gifted, minister in the Presbytery. He cares almost as little as she does for general company, though he is not put out by it. When they are together or among intimate friends, they are more rustic than ever. But the little bits of china which Bruce had ferreted out from odd holes and corners, the quaint spinning wheel which she had made Wat buy at the sale of a pauper's few old 'sticks of furniture,' Bruce's pretty arrangements with her baskets of flowers in the drawing-room and study, are piously preserved and lovingly kept up like the terrace and walk she designed in the garden as traces of her brief tenancy of the manse, and the love-dream of Wat Baillie's manhood.

And all that were not sent to Lily Kirkpatrick of the brood of bantams are fed regularly by the minister's own hand. They have the chance of becoming patriarchal fowls.

THE END.

www.ingramcontent.com/pod-product-compliance
Lightning Source LLC
Chambersburg PA
CBHW032149230426
43672CB00011B/2503